Collected Poems
Volume One

Just believe

Henry x

By the author

Staring Directly at the Eclipse

Travelling Second Class Through Hope

Raining Upwards

Art By Johnny ★

A Normal Family ♦

This Phantom Breath

The Department of Lost Wishes

Swallowing the Entire Ocean

Strikingly Invisible

The Escape Plan

The Beauty Within Shadow

The Distance Between Clouds

Collected Poems, Volume One

★ Collated and edited by Henry Normal
♦ With Angela Pell & published by Two Roads

HENRY NORMAL
COLLECTED POEMS
VOLUME ONE

Flapjack Press
flapjackpress.co.uk

Exploring the synergy between performance and the page

Published in 2021 by Flapjack Press
Salford, Gtr Manchester
⊕ flapjackpress.co.uk
🅵 Flapjack Press 🆈 FlapjackPress ▶ Flapjack Press

ISBN 978-1-8381185-6-3

All rights reserved
Copyright © Henry Normal, 2021
⊕ henrynormal.com
🅵 Henry Normal 🆈 HenryNormalpoet
📷 henrynormalpoet 📷 henrynormalpoetry

Cover art by Johnny Carroll-Pell
🅵 Art By Johnny 📷 johnnycarrollpell

Author photograph by Jim Holden
Courtesy of the author

Cover design by Paul Neads
⊕ paulneads.co.uk

Printed by Imprint Digital
Exeter, Devon
⊕ imprintdigital.com

This book is sold subject to the condition that is shall not by way of trade or otherwise be lent, re-sold, hired out or otherwise circulated in any form, binding or cover other than that in which it is published and without a similar condition including this condition being imposed on the subsequent purchaser.

*I would like to thank Linda Hallam, Penny Shepherd,
Ross Bradshaw, Theresa Sowerby, Colette Bryce,
Matt Welton, Paul Neads and my wife Angela Pell
for their help in bringing this collection together.*

Contents

Staring Directly at the Eclipse — 13

The breath within the balloon	15
If signatures reflect personality ...	16
I am not belittled by your culture of ambition	17
There is love at first sight	18
The house is not the same since you left	19
The missing page	20
The last parents	21
A prayer for the rejected	22
Skin	23
A gift	24
The frame of the Mona Lisa dreams	25
Photos with my son	26
Summer on Pluto	27
Logic is not a feeling	28
The eating of a unicorn	29
King Canute should have checked the tides	30
The first spark has led to this blaze	31
Animals and small children find me out	32
The perfect you	33
Cueva de las Manos	34
Abiogenesis to revelations	35
The joy of frogs	36
Beauty and the insect heart	37
If you should ever climb a tree	38
Uncomfortably positive	39
She is not looking at the camera	40
The questions they don't ask on the census	41
Should tenderness become plague	42
Staring directly at the eclipse	43
Is memory thought or emotion?	44
Beauty without numbers	46

This is not a house of war	47
Flux could kill	48
As if we could bottle this and take it with us	49
Saving me from monochrome	50
Sex and the kissing of salt	51
The dream ticket	52
Telegraph poles and ships' masts	54
Night fishing	55
A bed made into a city sightseeing tour bus	56
Tinned fruit and evaporated milk	57
The sleeping giant	58
Sand between the toes	59
Hidden chestnut at Herstmonceux	60
An acceptable use of an exclamation mark	61
The jar of joy	62
Beach of light	63
The wish list	64
Gravestones at a wedding	65
Windmills amongst almonds and oranges	66
When words are not your first language	67
Photo-bombing God	68
The ulterior motivator	70
A kind of loving	71
A view to die for	72
An offering to the people of the mounds	73
The fisherman of Alvor	74
Vanguard of audacious	75
The couple next door – a sharing experience	76
The heart of the last mammoth	78
The garden is still there underneath	79
Does a bad curtain call ruin a show?	80
A prayer for the hesitant	82
A message to my species	83

Travelling Second Class Through Hope	85
Embarrassed like the moon at midday	87
Sans pretension	88
The first time I died I was completely hopeless at it	89
Sitting on the idea of grass	90
She loves me, she loves me not	91
The Dinosaur War poems	92
Lying about your age	94
Never play chess with an anarcho-nihilist	95
Life after forever	96
Your room	97
A baby magpie	98
Concerning loss and theft	99
There will come a time you will no longer set aside …	100
Heavy Goods Vehicle	101
Stealing the scream	102
Skeleton	103
There is no need for the family to huddle round …	104
Welcome to the City of Self	105
Chapel of the Metal Shroud	106
Purity of spirit comes in all waist sizes	107
The reflection in the back of God's spoon	108
Ten ways to end a relationship	109
There's always room in the hearse on the way back	110
All kids are born with long thin moustaches	112
Travelling second class through Hope	113
Cornerhouse	114
Pragmatic romanticism	115
Only Christmas and birthdays bring death this close	116
The 44th minute	118
New friends tell me I've become disfigured in repartee	119
February	120
A more intimate fame	121
Within your arms	122
Why you never look like Paul Newman on family photos	123

The third person	124
Dopey and Juliet	125
Your elbow is close but you can't bite it	126
I am sitting with you again	127
Civic statues are never naked	128
In the open court of mountains like 12 angry jurors	129
Time passed unnoticed until she took the clock	130
Learning to understand the mechanics of the eclipse	132
The accidental death of a cat	133
No game show will ever hold your worth	134
A farce is still a farce even with subtitles	135
I turn my back when we've made love	136
Love – the disaster movie	137
Someone tossed a match into the corner of our past	138
Demoting Cupid to a chat show host	139
Hell is a place …	140
King Street	142
Mixed metaphors	143
Tomorrow's worms (a love poem to critics)	144
Recoiling from the anti-climax	145
Owning imperfection	146
Silence of the phone	147
When the time has come to leave	148
Mime doesn't pay	149
Your favourite mug	150
Breaking up is …	151
Beyond mathematics	152
She has given herself	153
I'm talking to someone else's father	154
When your eyes say 'I am here – is that not enough?'	155
Happiness	156
The lost generation of mermen and mermaids	157
Plain biscuits	158
A happy ending (revised)	159
To Helena and back	160
Love like Hell	161

Raining Upwards	163
The moon is leaving slowly	165
With zero the house always wins	166
Who wasn't out to sea didn't pray to God	167
Tunnelling into space	168
The Second Punic War is not available on a tea towel	169
As the ground accelerates towards you at an acute angle	170
"And wilt thou bend a listening ear to praises low as ours"	171
Walking away is made up of several moments	172
Voice of the ancient babirusa	173
A stream of consciousness meets the ocean	174
Nobody can remember who that is in the image	176
Fairy lights round a death bed	177
The remnants of a gymkhana	178
Altruism	180
Learning curves	181
An imaginary fly cannot be captured	182
Anchor	183
Sunglasses can make it seem darker than it actually is	184
Pictures of you without me	185
The canals of Mars at their height	186
Man in a glass booth	187
The smell of freshly cut grass is a communication	188
Twice as many hydrogen atoms as oxygen moving	189
"And can you then, who have such possessions …"	190
I'd like you to know	191
You've got me but who's got you?	192
Christmas at the end of the old world	193
Academia and the compulsion to compete	194
Fame as a perpetual wedding	195
Audition for Heaven	196
Exploring rockpools	197
Horizontal amid horticulture	198
This season of new life	199
Raining upwards	200

Hominin footprints in Laetoli	202
Are other animals afraid of their own species?	203
Electric like a tree praising the sky	204
Deafness and social cohesion	205
Evident	206
There's more to lemons than being yellow	207
Unmarked	208
If you never saw this tree it must be difficult to imagine …	209
Soaking	210
The self-deception of priority	211
The spiral staircase casts a shadow	212
The March of Progress	213
At the hearth of the winter sky	214
Travelling in 4D	215
Slitting my own throat	216
Auditioning for the X-men in the Wetlands	217
Without trespass	218
Windswept and drunk on oxygen	219
Orphan	220
Pilgrimage for the agnostic	221
Headland	222
Guadolupe and the navigator	223
This is a likeness of things that no longer exist	224
The sheet music of Microwave Background Radiation	225
Sand suspended in mid-air	226
Eskimo kiss	227
The foghorn has long since given up	228
What would I have done better?	230
Exquisite	231
The movement of shadows on the moon	232
First prize	234
You won't find a box to tick on any form for this	235
This is merely blossom, fruit will follow	236
Leakage	237
There is a ghost on the shoreline taking a selfie	238

As though infinity could be turned off	239
The difference between falling down and having a fall	240
Sofa at the centre of the constellation	241
The walking wounded at Lidl	242
Vibrations	244
Earth reclaims the threshold	245
The intoxication of tidal shift	246
Before moving into the heart of a new lawn	247
Landed	248
The shaded garden	249
Kissing the top of my own head	250
There are layers of cloud moving in different directions	251
This is a photo of me not smiling	252
A little slope of meadow outside my window	253
Altamura Neanderthal	254
The stone mask	255
I've never had an email worth keeping forever	256
Reclaimed	257
Pivot	258
Self-portrait of the poet as an old man	259
Near miss	260
Hold me with certainty in this heavenly chaos	262
Late renewal	263
Witness	264
Moon in the morning sky	265

STARING DIRECTLY
AT THE ECLIPSE

The breath within the balloon

The breath within the balloon will not last
You never get inflated balloons
on the *Antiques Road Show*
Breath brings with it vulnerability

If never inflated
a balloon may last forever
but such limp reason
will never enchant a child
with decoration
or gladden the heart
with the stretching of possibility
and the fulfilment of promise

Is not a universe of such balloons sadder
than a universe where balloons are apt to burst?

I hold your breath within my hands

The breath within the balloon will not last
but the giving of breath
and the tying of the knot
at each new birth
is an offering
for our choice of worlds

If signatures reflect personality they cannot all remain constant

It's not that I've forgotten my own name
it's just that my signature doesn't flow naturally like it used to

I hesitate as the pen blotches the first ink, self-conscious
Each letter has become foreign, a random code of symbols

With deliberate forgery I have to match up my commitment
with a genuine signature that has already been approved

I'm cribbing off my own past

It's as if my signature is trying to change but is restrained
by the functional need of the authorised version

Strange how we set our own guidelines, our own parameters
so early for something so permanent

I remember practising my signature as a teenager
I'm sure I never understood this was to remain
unchanged forever

As a result my signatures have become clumsy
like a child's crayon letters

I suppose I'm worried if I just sign a new signature
this will not be accepted

Is it possible to authorise a change of signature?
How will I sign for it?

I am not belittled by your culture of ambition

My wife has a moustache
It is plastic
It came out of a Christmas cracker

We are monarchy
in our paper hats

I am King Superman in his favourite cardigan
full of pud

It's not a thought-through image
we are ramshackle
a homely mess
like bric-a-brac
at a car boot

There is no sleekness to our design
no colour coordination
no concession to taste

Against all rules of fashion
and all aesthetic consideration
we are happy
at ease
daft in love

There is love at first sight

There is wonder in attraction
the dancing of light on the retina
the alignment of atoms into form and substance
the perception of science as nature

Anatomy and biology raised to aesthetics and beauty
the tautness of flesh over muscle and frame
the way fabric clings to an outline
the contours of a ribcage
the tilt of a pelvis
the enticement of hollows and shadows
poise and the grace of texture

Colours and tones that blend and sculpt the imagination
the vulnerability of a neckline
the fragrance of moisture and the lure of intoxication
the glow of touch and the genius of the blood's energy
there is miracle in personality
there is wonder in attraction
there is love at first sight
I am already yours

The house is not the same since you left

The house is not the same since you left
the cooker is angry – it blames me
The TV tries desperately to stay busy
but occasionally I catch it staring out of the window
The washing up's feeling sorry for itself again
it just sits there saying 'What's the point, what's the point?'
The curtains count the days
Nothing in the house will talk to me
I think your armchair's dead
The kettle tried to comfort me at first
but you know what its attention span's like
I've not told the plants yet
they still think you're on holiday
The bathroom misses you
I hardly see it these days
it still can't believe you didn't take it with you
The bedroom won't even look at me
since you left it keeps its eyes closed
all it wants to do is sleep, remembering better times
trying to lose itself in dreams
it seems like it's taken the easy way out
but at night I hear the pillows
weeping into the sheets

The missing page

and it made a mockery of the rest

and it became the most important of all pages

and neither of us could write a replacement

and we could never agree on its contents
only sometimes in broad outline

and there were times when we denied it had ever existed
and times when I believed it to be several pages

and it became the perfect excuse

and the amount we attributed to it could never be contained on
a single sheet

and if only the pages had never been numbered

and

The last parents

Huddled around
the very last sun
a final handful of humans
try yet again to create
one artificial star that will survive

The parents telling that same story
of how the sky once dazzled with a million suns

How
as
one by one the lights went out
generation after generation
traced a path like a dot-to-dot
to this
the final glimmer

And how once there were as many souls
in the universe as there were these stars

And how their parents had told them
this story when they were young

And how their parents had told them
not to be afraid of the dark

A prayer for the rejected

we start from nothing and build
and you may
judge down from perfection

catalogue all that we are not
measure against legends and aeons
ignore mitigation

dismiss originality as untested
discard handcrafted as unprofessional
destroy with a whim

discount our unborn
belittle our dreams
and despite all this

again
we start from nothing and build

Skin

More skin than I could possibly need
has been arriving at my door now for weeks
There is no return address

I've tried giving it away to friends
but they have no use for it

I've taken out ads in the local paper
I've even tried car boot sales
but there seems to be a glut in the market at the moment

I had a word with the Post Office
but there's nothing they can do

I'm running out of storage space
I can no longer get my car in the garage

I've secretly tried dumping bin bags full at night
but I swear the same skin arrives back in the morning
together with the standard delivery

In desperation I burnt several layers in the back garden
but the neighbours complained
and a man from the council called round and said
I was causing a health risk

I'm resigned to carrying as much as I can about with me now
It's all I can think to do

I can see people staring at me
pitying me
whispering behind my back
asking if I can breathe under all that skin

I could post the skin onto someone else
like a chain letter
but I wouldn't wish this on anyone

A gift

At 7 o'clock this morning
I bring you a mountain
I tap gently on your window
and you wake half covered in sleep

"What's that?" you ask
"It's a mountain" I grin
"I've carried it all night
I couldn't sleep so I brought it here to show you"

"What do I want with a mountain in my garden
at 7 o'clock in the morning?" you ask
not used to being woken at 7 o'clock
with a mountain in your garden

I try to joke, now feeling a little embarrassed

"It's for you, a gift"
You say you don't want a mountain
You are too tired to understand
and I struggle to explain

it's not the mountain I've brought you
it's the fact that I could bring it to you
I strain to pick it up again
and wonder what I'm going to do with it now

I feel such a fool walking home with a mountain

The frame of the Mona Lisa dreams

Though you have looked in my direction many times
you do not remember me
Hung on a wall on my own
you would not exalt me

I have intrinsic value

but this notoriety is not of my own making
I have seen eyes filled with wonder glance over me

Like the plain sister
I see all
but am not seen
The curious and the cynical I see
the desperate and the disappointed

Like the assassin my fame is a reflection
like the bodyguard I am expendable
I know my place at court

And in all the borrowed light shined upon me
from my vantage at the edge of the glare
occasionally I see refracted
in the tiring of a gaze
something of myself

A gentle sob
almost, yet not quite, lost

Remember me
it seems to say

Remember me
and I will remember you

Photos with my son

Johnny is not interested in having his
photo taken

When prompted he will look at the lens
His hand is likely to move at any moment

I suspect he is not sure what is expected of him
"Smile" he says

He doesn't smile
he just says smile

echoing the words
from behind the camera

Summer on Pluto

In a room with no windows
I am given a leaflet

The word incurable
is printed in bold on the first page

This is the only time I will spend in this room
This is the only time I will speak to this person

Autism is a spectrum
there are degrees

Your son is mildly severe
What does that mean?

It means he will always live at home
it means he will never have a job

never have a girlfriend
never be capable of taking care of himself

You will never have a conversation with him
ever

It means you will worry about him everyday
you will worry if he's happy

you will worry if he's lonely
you will worry what will happen to him when you die

Mildly severe
benignly savage

kindly cruel
none of this appeared on the leaflet

Logic is not a feeling

The horizon out to sea
feels like the nearest nature gets to
a straight line

Seen from any one coast
the curve is slight

There is comfort
in the simplicity
of such a vast uninterrupted skyline

Something peaceful
in the lack of clutter

With a cloudless sky
and very little wave
the meeting of the light and royal blue
is perfection

You can be forgiven
for thinking that if you go beyond this reach
you fall

adrift without compass

The eating of a unicorn

So I'm eating this unicorn and I'm thinking
this isn't right
but you've got to eat haven't you?

So you tell yourself it's OK
everybody eats them
but you know that's not strictly true

So you look for some justification, some strand of logic
some attitude, some philosophy, however slim
but you know in your gut it still isn't right

So you think about minimising the damage
but you know you can't simply throw up and piece the whole
business back together

So you say what is done is done and you have to live with it
but you still wish you hadn't eaten the bloody thing
and wonder how you could have ever felt that hungry

So you pretend it never happened
that you know nothing about it
and besides, you thought it was just a horse made up
but now you have to dispose of what's left of the body
and in case it's discovered
you have to hide the head and the horn separately

So there you are, breaking off the head and the horn
from a half-eaten unicorn at dead of night
but

King Canute should have checked the tides

Taking your own chair to the beach
is a commitment
fleecy on
hood up

Better to keep your limbs moving
some might say
but sitting is a definite statement

We are not just passing through
we are making a stand
sitting firm

Day trippers we are not
nor ill prepared tourists
We are stones amongst scattered pebbles
rocks amongst shingle

Bring on your highest wave
the glory is ours
we live here
we own this weather

The first spark has led to this blaze

All stories are universal
All told from a unique point of view

This is the universe
at this moment
from this perspective

Whether you want to or not
you represent life

You are what life looks like
at this instant
from this vantage
from inside the vast array

The story of life
the story of creation witnessed
from the first spark
to the disintegration of the very last cell
is one story
our story

Whether you are interested enough
to engage or not
or brave enough
to contribute further
you are already part of the narrative

At this pulse
from a collusion of all that has gone before
you are life
you are the universe

you are the story

Animals and small children find me out

It is not that I am of no worth
just that I've managed to exaggerate my worth

or at least I've allowed my worth to be exaggerated
beyond my ability to pretend justification

Animals and small children find me out

I don't even keep plants around the house nowadays
I had hoped to live up to this flattery

but it becomes a chore
like constantly walking around on tiptoes

and sooner or later you wonder
at the true benefit of the extra height

The perfect you

I am the other you
the perfect you
the one bred from your DNA
taken at birth
our birth
cultivated for spare parts
kept alive by machines
stored in the dark
waiting

We grow simultaneous
alike but not quite
for I have no defects
no scars
no scratches
no weathered skin
no blemishes
no bruises
no acquired resistance
no yellowing of the eye
no tooth decay
no furrows in the brow
no creases on the palms

no lifeline
no loveline

I am the other you
the perfect you

Cueva de las Manos

I place my left hand
on that most solid

Spread out my fingers
to form a stencil

Blow kaolin and manganese
through hollow bone
to leave a silhouette

Whether we call it art
or human nature

on every continent
something survives

vulnerable as dust

Over two thousand generations call
each with a simple statement
as urgent as blood through veins

I am here
I am here
I am here

Abiogenesis to revelations

Twenty watts amid all this vitality

My one descendant
holds a dinosaur up to the sunset
We are engaged in an exchange of energy

Half the stars in the Milky Way
shine inside this precious three pounds

Electromagnetic radiation hitting the retina
fires the optic nerve
with the enormity of creation

The alchemy of emotion overwhelms
The ache infinite

I'm told
there are no numbers or names in nature
existence is independent of the mind

love and beauty
just icons on a computer screen

I am overawed by every single atom
Moments like this I could believe in God
Moments like this I could kiss him

The joy of frogs

Frogs need kisses like anyone else

Not all of them want to become handsome princes
some prefer a more pond-based lifestyle

What if you turn into a handsome prince
and the princess really prefers frogs?

What if you're not that handsome a prince?
Maybe you're more handsome a frog?

Let's face it, chances are
if you can get kissed fairly regularly by a princess
and remain a frog
you've got it made

If she gives you tongues
then go for it

Beauty and the insect heart

The ocean is the wisest of counsellors
Before its double moon
comforted by a mother's breath
I offer my heart as a small gift of stones

This is the closest I may get to perfection
I saw a thousand shoes today but one pair of eyes
They've discovered over a million stars
but so far only one planet with life

Some distance along the shoreline
I can see a young couple
They are easy and familiar
They have something
all my sullen romance cannot reach

There is no urgency now
only the hurting of a single truth

I would give everything, everything
to share such acceptance
Not just with anyone, not just in abstract
but vivid like the cleansing of pain
or the healing of fractured bone

Here I will soothe the night
Here I will help build a cathedral of words

not for worship or inanimate passion
or another broken relic on a forgotten mound
but for someone, someone close, knelt alone
somewhere on a distant beach
offering her heart as a small gift of stones

Later, nursing the motorway north and home
the sunrise whispers promises in a rear-view mirror

If you should ever climb a tree

I'm not sure how much weight
my head can support

but I enjoy the familiarity
the casual lack of boundaries

Without a word
we get a sense of someone

If you should ever climb a tree
I will be your low hanging branch
I want that to be unquestioned

If my neck snaps
it was meant to be

It is the most important thing
to know

In the absence of sufficient language
I would rather seek out trees
to remind you

Uncomfortably positive

This might not seem that different a picture to you
but this is the look of a mother
to her autistic child
taking his first photo

The look of a mother
anticipating success

the coalface of optimism
the body language of hope

If I was susceptible to joy
this could easily affect me

Unlike my wife
I have immunity
to all forms of jubilation

I err towards caution
bordering scepticism
on matters of good fortune or progress

This condition we embrace
I've learnt is not linear
not predictable like neurotypical behaviour

Five minutes after you leave us
you will turn to one another and say
"Well, we can see where that comes from"

She is not looking at the camera

She is not looking at the camera
What can she see?
There's something off
a thought, a memory
There's a hint of a smile
but a faraway sadness in her eyes

Am I projecting
or sensitive to disparity?
Singling out the one expression amid the group
disregarding the set instruction
There is the suspicion of sea in the distance
All detail of sky is lost in monochrome

Heavy clothes suggest
the weather is bracing
but these were the days of formality
even on the promenade
Where are you?
Yours is the thought that intrigues me

It's easy to look into the camera
It's what is expected
Isn't the unexpected more interesting though?
Somehow more beautiful
more human
a quiet blow for a world of other

The questions they don't ask on the census

Hands up anyone
who is lonely
or has ever felt loneliness?

Anyone who has hidden themselves away
on New Year's Eve
rather than face that hiatus
of emptiness in public?

Anyone who has dressed up
on a Saturday night
and forced themselves out
into the melee
only to return home
having not spoken to a single soul?

Anyone who has searched faces on the pavement
for a fragment of recognition?

Anyone who has stood at the edge of a window in hope?

Anyone who has touched a photo in remembrance?

Anyone who has put a pillow behind them in the dark
against the cold?
Anyone who finds a mirror the hardest place to look
or lowers their eyes when they meet someone?

Anyone who aches without knowing what for?
Anyone afraid of being found wanting?

Should tenderness become plague

Should tenderness become plague
glory in its infection
carry its contagion
and pray the germ is hereditary

Staring directly at the eclipse

Your feet on my lap
as we settle for the night

A shoreline to ourselves
Sunlight on water

Nature catching the eye unexpected
Fresh air intoxicating

Getting lost in art or endeavour
Music that carries and caresses

Food presented as a gift
Being surprised by genius or kindness

Your face flush and immediate
A friendly soul at my window

Hope in all forms however tiny
The comforting mundanity of doing nothing much

The absence of pain and fear
however fleeting

A familiar arm around my shoulder
The satisfaction of something done well

Loyalty and honour embraced
Minor revelations of perception

The defiance within spirit against overwhelming odds
Valour and grace in the face of the inevitable

To spite death
and make his victory hollow

Is memory thought or emotion?

Monkey bin
is a huge monkey head on a bin

It's not a real monkey
it doesn't move or make a noise
it has no arms or legs or body
just a head on top of a waste bin

This is Johnny's favourite bit of the zoo
Mine too

Johnny did like the penguins
It's a relief to know what he likes
or doesn't like
it's probably the basis of all
personality

He hates erratic noise
dogs and babies or
young girls who can't get what they want

I was drawn to the infant giraffes
awkward and strangely poetic
Johnny wasn't impressed
the moment came and went

The tiger intimidated
I could see in his eyes
he'd fuck me up if he could

I'm sure there were other animals
real monkeys and shit
but the only animals I remember
apart from monkey bin

are the giraffes, the tiger and
the penguins
and what I felt when I saw them

It's more the feeling I recall
and a yearning
for connection

Beauty without numbers

Presented with Colour by Numbers
he chooses only what colour he wants
only what borders appeal

The figurative made abstract
The shape of the world embellished

New edges imagined
The palette reinvigorated

A choice is braved
A universe decided
Personality shaming mathematics

Lines enhanced as never before
to create
a map of self-determination

This is not a house of war

Everything I want for my children
I want for your children

Everything I wish for me
I wish for you

This is not a house of fear
This is a house of life

How can I not see myself in you
If you look
how can you not see yourself in me

You are respected as much as I am
You are of worth in equal measure

You are family
You are us

This is not a house of intolerance
This is a house of acceptance

We are the house
You and I

This is where you belong
This is where we belong

This is your home
This is our home

Flux could kill

Two feet from certain death
Two feet of existence
not menacing but matter-of-fact
The choice is always as narrow as this
only here
you can measure spirit

The grass leans outward
The cliff
jagged with purpose
penetrates the waves

Two feet of lies and soft options
Two feet of fear and pulse
There is a truth that's too easy to forget until you fill your
lungs with determination

At times such as dusk
there is wonder in the commonplace

Rain hangs on the skyline
Beauty is always this short a distance

I have spent my whole life trying to enter the gates of Heaven
using my heart as a battering ram

Two feet of the attainable
Two feet from acceptance

As if we could bottle this and take it with us

We travel as far as the Romans
to recreate home

A simple meal
elegance without formality

Trees surround our table
like the quietest of staff

There is a scent of eucalyptus
a distant fountain underscores

Early afternoon
softened by leaves

The world is busy elsewhere
scorpions on an open fire

Nature pays us no mind
we breathe our own space

We bathe in the spring
and dance on hand-paved stone

We are invisible
to all but ourselves

Saving me from monochrome

I have no qualifications
no legitimacy
no foundation
I do have a chunky computer

I am dressing down
industrial

I am trying
I am trying to be serious
I am trying hard to be serious
I am trying too hard to be serious
like the metallic grey bricks behind us

You are smiling
leaning into me
but in reality
I am leaning into you

Sex and the kissing of salt

The rhapsody of gesture
a covenant of nature

a merging of fluids and gentleness
the homage of caress

the warmest gift
a mutual worship

the applauding of skin
the salutation within

the sincerest poetry
the perfect society

the reverence of the body's grace
the innermost embrace

the enchantment of response
the harmony of imbalance

the threshold of adoration
the theatre of captivation

a more intimate fame
the empathy bargain

the exaltation of the senses
the camaraderie of indulgences

the ballad of creation
the divine celebration
the glory of immersion

The dream ticket

Man with obvious disability in maintaining relationships seeks all-consuming passion but will settle for friendship and the occasional shag. Doesn't believe relationships ever work but has been known to fake undue optimism.

Woman must be classic beauty, half saint half whore (ONO). Must be 100 per cent loyal but tolerant of bumbling indiscretion. Must have no friends that she wouldn't ditch just to spend a few extra seconds in my presence.

Must be available to lavish attention on me whenever I need pampering but have interesting things to do when I'm busy so that I can be entertained when we next meet.

Must have no friends that are male, unless they are grossly ugly. All female friends should be incredibly horny and desperate to sleep with me given the slightest chance.

Must be caring and gentle in bed but willing to be ravished, tied up and have various substances smeared over specific portions of the anatomy. Must cum very loudly every time we have sex. Must synchronise with each of my orgasms. Must groan and moan softly until the final stages then shout such comments as "I've never had it so good", "You're so big" and "God, I love you".

Must burst into tears for no reason occasionally and when challenged say "I don't want to lose you".

Must hate every one of my male friends. Find them sexually repulsive and inferior to me in every way. Must understand that my female friends are just friends and that's different.

Must always have a worse time than me at parties. Must hate parties, students, arty wankers, wanky art students, parties with wanky art students.

Must be completely naïve, innocent and optimistic but worldly wise. Must be young at heart but sensible. Must be practically a virgin but have a sophisticated knowledge of sexual technique.

Must be intelligent but not so that it makes me realise my simplistic thought processes.

Most importantly must realise that all the above is not a joke.

Please send tasteful nude photo.

Telegraph poles and ships' masts

Telegraph poles and ships' masts
are hard to tell apart
from a distance

We are sitting on a wall
by the harbour

With my golfing hat on
you can't see the onset of grey
or tell that I don't play golf

With Johnny's arm around his mum
you might not tell he's autistic
even at 17

Although the wooden Pinocchio
he holds to his face
might make you question

If you look closely telegraph poles
are connected
whereas ships' masts aren't

as ships sail away in different directions

Night fishing

You can choose to give these mountains
any name you want
at this moment they are yours

To the north
    no sign of human habitation
untamed ridges muted blue and grey
backlit with a peach haze

To the east
    a line of street lights
marks out civilisation
like a landing strip

To the south
    across the plasma screen
of the lake's surface
beacons appear on the slopes
and reflect
like the tracks of tears

To the west
    the lap of the wake
a moored yacht sways so gently
as if to lull a baby to sleep

At the heart
    in a small rowboat
a man and his son
sit and fish
in water from the ice age
silent as a distant star

We are greater than gods tonight
we are life

A bed made into a city sightseeing tour bus

On your left you will see
a boy who only plays with adults

Though he's sitting in the driving seat
he has his back to the steering wheel

Teddy bears are passengers
the wheels are paper plates

Someone has gone to a bit of trouble

But the bus is only visible from the outside
Inside it requires imagination

or the retention of the view from the outside
or is the little boy just sitting in his bed

behind a handmade barrier?

Tinned fruit and evaporated milk

So it was last Saturday teatime when I called in at my dad's
He was sat checking his racing results
I ambled across the room and turned off the TV

"Just a second" I said tentatively before he started to protest
"I've got something important to tell you"

I hesitated a moment, then bracing myself I came right out with it
"I love you dad"

"Don't be so bloody daft" he said

"It's not daft" I said, "I love you"

"Err… alright" he said, "put kettle on"

"No, you're supposed to say 'I love you too son', c'mon dad you've seen *Dallas*"

"I've not got time for all this bloody nonsense, I'm off to the Legion" he said

So I'm following him down the garden and I'm saying
"Look dad, I'm in my fifties now and I think it's about time
it was out in the open
I love you"

And he's trying to *shh* me in case the neighbours hear

So I shout louder "I don't care if the whole world hears,
I'm not ashamed of my feelings, I love you, you're my dad"
And I give him a big wet kiss on the forehead
"What do you say dad, what do you say?"

"Oh Henry" he said, "where did I go wrong?"

The sleeping giant

You lift your face to the open sky
and lie with the sediment
where the sea and stones have come to an accord

And you wonder how you couldn't have
known about this place before

It existed before
and you existed
and now you are aware

And this could be your favourite place
as though the elements had conspired
to fashion and fit your shape

And to think you almost didn't turn that corner
that you had become tired of corners

doubted their promise

And suddenly a world of corners surprises
presents possibility
adventure
illumination
hope

Sand between the toes

This is what constitutes an action shot in my world

The thinning at my crown is conveniently out of frame
The avalanche under my chin obscured

If I have a best side, this is it

According to my father-in-law's socks it's Monday
The mid-west easiness to his attire betrays no irony
other than that he's from Peterborough

Johnny shows the least interest in having his feet cleaned
He'd make a good pharaoh
nonchalant during de-sanding
ear defenders and fiddly bit of plastic now part of the ensemble

I use his red sock like a shoe-shine boy
buffing the digits

My mother-in-law relaxes leaning forward
her walking sticks hook the bench
like stabilisers

Autistic Family Robinson

Even behind a camera my wife is the centre

If she dies first
we will be buried alive in her tomb
we just don't know it yet

Hidden chestnut at Herstmonceux

Outliving the royal houses of Europe
sweetness, cultivated by humans

We are children beneath your branches
paying tribute

We've returned to stand at your root
and let you know you are not forgotten

As generations have passed
there is no footfall here
but explorers and pilgrims

Though we only stop a while
sought with affection
favourites are understood

The decades are long
the seconds too short

We are holding up
seeing old friends
sharing time with family

An acceptable use of an exclamation mark

Johnny looks good in a hat
not self-conscious

I'm always wondering if I should
take a hat off when I go indoors

Johnny is definite
if he's keeping it on, that's it

I'm guessing he's deciding what he wants
not what you think about it

He came over to me
yesterday

and put his arm around my shoulder
for a second

Then he said
"Daddy to go"

I said
"You came over to me!"

but those are my rules
not his

The jar of joy

No amount of sugar can preserve it
A euphoric surge unscheduled unable to sustain

Freak weather within the soul
A guest that's always welcome but seldom turns up

Giving back control to the cosmos
for but a breath

Unsettled by an overwhelming gratitude for being
Momentarily in love with the whole bloody mess

The perfect wave in a restless surf
A sudden realisation of possibility

Optimism made tangible for an instant
A fresh breeze through an open heart

Beach of light

Surveying the sand sculptures on Luz beach
I'm reminded of Ozymandias, King of Kings
Look on my works, ye Mighty and despair!

There is a two-foot pyramid, a hippo and a child-friendly T. rex
an over-sized snail and other animals I can't quite make out
Johnny drops a euro into the man's hat
from such a height it can easily be mistaken for attitude

We share the tide with a starfish
The moon finds its way through cloud

Balancing on a rock
lifting one leg at a time
we toy with gravity and its eventual victory

I straighten my back
lift my head as high as I can
Not yet you've got me, not yet

The wish list

To arrive at a place
where the past has no pain

where frailty is accepted

where all is beauty
immediate, important
connected, indivisible
exquisite

The greatest show in the universe
and you with a front seat
and you are the star

and everything is Life
and Life is everything
and you are Life
and you are everything

To arrive at a place
where all is cherished
and you are cherished
and you
cherish yourself
and breathe

and breathe

Gravestones at a wedding

Before God
we are outsiders on the edge

We can appear to fit in
until you look closely

My watch hangs from my wrist
My wife's dress displays birds in flight

My boy leans against the cold stone
head down

We are not really here
or we're too here

Awkward
self-conscious

Not knowing the rules
not understanding what is expected of us

Mirroring, echoing
not knowing where our edges are

Hesitant ghosts
checking our invitations

Windmills amongst almonds and oranges

Trees stripped of cork cover the slopes
straggling the crest like
stray hairs on the back of an old man's neck

Alien on hills of metallic blue
a giant tai chi class
waves in greeting

Stood in cool formation
like a *Reservoir Dogs* poster
windmills amongst almonds and oranges

These sleek prefects lord it
with a serene semaphore
nobility in the mist

Such synchronised grace reminds me of
pensioners moving in the edges of the sea

When words are not your first language

Any parent would sooner be ill
than their child

There is a helplessness

Johnny can't quite get the hang
of blowing his nose

His top lip gets raw
like bacon hitting the pan
I wince
and close my eyes to steel myself

Strangely he allows
more contact when poorly
he loses his edges
his lovableness is irresistible

Patience and distraction
are the only prescription

His mum throws her heart
into bamboozling him
through the worst

with such attention and diversion
we could call it just an everyday devotion

There are no words for what passes here

Photo-bombing God

A palm is four fingers
A foot is four palms
A cubit is six palms
Four cubits make a man

My son's skin is almost prepubescent perfect
sideburns suggesting maturity awaits

From the sacred to the unanchored
a sequence of genes mutate

geometry
is remapped

I'm resigned to the thinning of grey
a turning stubble hides my scars

Johnny is far cooler in his sunglasses
he wears a straw hat with the ease of a teenager

Nucleic acid replaces architectural design
twenty-three chromosome pairs roll

I've shaved my eyebrow in the middle
so as not to resemble a Neanderthal

We are a little burnt by the sun
I can't believe my face was once as small as his

The tree of life twists in a double helix
the canon of proportions spiral

I look into the camera because I know it's expected
and one of us has to

Johnny still displays no compulsion to conform
he has no interest in consequence

Two thousand two hundred hopes disorder
The Archangel's detail is without error

A pace is four cubits
A man is twenty-four palms
A man is twenty thousand five hundred proteins coding
A man is three billion pairs of chance

The ulterior motivator

I've looked for you
all my adult life

in the proudest of my achievements
in the embarrassment of my shortcomings

in the possibilities of every relationship
in the eye contact of every stranger

in the opening of every door
from the window of every train
on every horizon out to sea

in loud and smoke-filled rooms
over the rim of every glass

across every public gathering
down the line of every queue

in the glare of every headlight
in every face of every crowd

in the most bleak of landscapes
in the closing of every curtain

I've looked for you

A kind of loving

She came home one day and he'd gone
In his favourite chair he'd left a yoghurt
Unaccustomed to change
she lived with the yoghurt for three years
It never moved from the chair
They slept apart
She often wondered if there was someone else
It never ate what she served up
It ignored relatives
She would often have to hoover round it
Her sister-in-law told her she was barmy
to stick it out this long
But she knew that marriage was something you had to work at
She went to marriage guidance on her own
until they said they could do nothing further
if the yoghurt didn't accompany her on
the next visit
Eventually she packed her bags and left
It was a hard decision
You can't live with a yoghurt for three years
without it leaving its mark on your life
She had some fond memories though
of those early days
and kept a photo of the yoghurt amongst her letters

A view to die for

If this balcony collapses I am extinct

but it is a risk I take casually
this ageless vista is essential
to a life wholly lived

When my wife and son join me
I am a little more conscious of odds
and consequences

When he starts banging the side
I begin to feel increasingly mortal
the scenery becoming less vital with each blow

An offering to the people of the mounds

I am wearing hand-me-downs from my son
at the edge of these white cliffs
where the grass is at its greenest

We are an army of one
three heads
six arms
strong in faith and valour

Our passion is unrecorded
in the book of invasions

Our small rebellion
may not be legend

but imagination is the greatest freedom
and no matter how poor
you can always afford ancestors

I wave farewell
from Niall of the Nine Hostages
from the crossbowman on the battlements
from the sons of Míl Espáine

We are here amongst the cormorants
we have reached this isle of destiny
we are the Angel of the South

Poetry is all around us and within us
This is a land of abundance
as holy as we believe

Lost amid the cloud
descendant of the High Kings

The fisherman of Alvor

There is a dinosaur
unconcerned by our presence

He is waiting upon his prey
black wings outstretched for balance
patient as the grim reaper

His reflection in the water is an anchor
the inlet gunmetal grey
ripples iron filings

Loaded clouds move like tectonic plates
I am sitting with your mother, unsteady

We are temporary
Vulnerable

Too human to settle in this chill landscape
we walk a little to warm the blood

Vanguard of audacious

Kindness is bravery at its brazen best
its boldest and most ballsy

It empowers all it touches

To put your heart in the line of fire
is as heroic as it is honourable

To be gentle you offer up a vulnerable underbelly
Empathy and humanity are gifts that entail risk

No matter how everyday it may seem
to dare to act not in self-interest
is valiant

To demand dignity for others undaunted is intrepid

To find strength to confront and challenge prejudice requires courage
however uncool to cynics

To make a stand for justice, equality and even love
is never unfashionable, never untimely

To insist that tenderness endures and that mercy is victorious
you put your body above the parapet

To face injury, loss, ridicule or one of a hundred fears
but still have resolve and compassion
is a testament to an indomitable spirit

On whatever scale
the matter-of-factness of such nobility
is a quiet but magnificent defiance

The couple next door – a sharing experience

The couple in the flat next door are always considerate enough to save their arguments until it's time for bed.

This selfless gesture ensures that their intimate secrets, their sexual inadequacies, inferiority and persecution complexes, petty jealousies, childhood traumas, parental rejections, adolescent failings, perverse lust fantasies, unfulfilled animal needs and their constant insecurity in the other's commitment to the relationship are all that much easier for us to enjoy.

The annoying thing is though that he insists on whimpering in a weak pathetic whine that's very difficult to make out. She on the other hand has perfect diction through a rising scale from full pitch screaming right up to violent hysterical frenzy, at which she is particularly entertaining. It seems a general rule for both that the logic content of the argument decreases in direct proportion to the volume and speed of delivery. Another annoying habit he has is that of speaking away from the adjoining wall and I get the feeling sometimes that he's a little embarrassed at what he's actually saying. She however grasps every opportunity to exploit this weakness and gain the upper hand by repeating his sentences word for word in the form of a very loud exclamation.

A problem they share jointly is the frequent compulsion to storm off into another room after a particularly good line. Other distractions include the unnecessarily long pauses often mistaken for a premature aborting of the conflict leaving both participants and audience alike with a frustrating sense of anti-climax, and the sporadic fits of door-banging that can so often surprise even the most careful of listeners, causing any glass not firmly held to make that embarrassing smashing sound as it drops from your ear to the foot of the wall.

Possibly the most pitifully pathetic and therefore the most interesting phase of the argument usually comes when he's ready to make up but she's not quite ready. For the next six or seven minutes he's apologetic and condescending, then after one too many rejections he suddenly blows his top stomping around and shouting such memorable classics as "I'm trying to be nice to you, you stupid prat!".

I don't think he's actually ever hit her though she's been violent, often unnervingly violent, many times, but once I understand, in desperation trying to disperse the anger, he spat full in her face. You could tell from the immediate reaction that he knew even as it happened it was the worst thing he could do. Listening to two broken people crying in the night can suddenly make you feel very lonely. At this point I usually hug my girlfriend tight and thank God that tonight the argument was next door.

The heart of the last mammoth

Not even on prime time TV
but on the minority interest channel
I saw a scientist break open the heart of a mammoth
"It is very rare" he said
"There are only two in existence"

We were never told if
the other mammoth's heart
had yet been broken

The garden is still there underneath

Red trousers draw the eye
like blood on the snow
or stigmata on a holy shroud

It's hard in the wide shot
to tell who is present

We are rolling winter
My hands are stinging
my son's must be

White is the predominant colour
dark green and brown compete with black
like a stencil

Bleak but with majesty
this is our world
this is us
We are where we belong

Even in the coldest of breath
we have our own beauty
it doesn't shout
it is noise intolerant

Those footprints in the snow
they are ours

Does a bad curtain call ruin a show?

I'm never any good at goodbyes

I feel too much pressure
to produce some sort of fitting climax
As though fulfilling a duty or observing the
constraints of an art form

It's the unalterable finality
I feel looming like a punchline
you know is not going to work

A polite thank you and goodnight
never seems sufficient

We expect

He'll pull something from up his sleeve you'll see
It'll end with a bang, the big finale
It's not over till the fat lady sings

He'll have held something special back
Always save the best till last
Wait for the fireworks, there's bound to be fireworks

I'm stood at the door again
having said all I've got to say, having had a great time
nervous that I could spoil it all in three seconds

Am I the only one who feels
there's too much onus on the notion of climax?
Am I lacking in stamina, character, goodwill?

Are people so fickle
that the last thing you say colours every other gesture?

Are people's memories so short they cannot cast their minds back
to five or ten minutes before the end?

I can never kiss that much more
than I kissed at the height of my passion

I can never wave that better wave
exert that extra effort
surpass everything that's gone before

So a thank you and goodnight will have to suffice

Of course
if I do happen to make a grand exit
two minutes later I have to return
having forgotten my hat

A prayer for the hesitant

A pale blue dot
amid a family portrait

This is your home planet
you are where you were born to be
breathe

The world is your living room
you are amongst friends
your ancestors, your family and
over ten thousand saints look down

Nobody means you any harm
not even God or nature
you can choose not to fear

The universe expects nothing
Every single thing is more than nothing
You have already exceeded expectation

If you forget me
my name
this moment
remember only this
you are good enough

imperfect as we are
you are good enough

A message to my species

I will not live on
my son will be the last of me
my evolutionary line is going out in a blaze of indifference

I quite like that
our little joke on the selfish gene
our snub to the scramble
for permanence and immortality

The rest of the universe will just have to get on
without me and my family
and our genetic material

This is the summit of our possibility
the culmination of millions of years' preparation
a wondrous cascade of consequence
a glorious accident embraced

Thank you life
thank you universe
we'll have the best time we can

then you are on your own
Try not to fuck it up

TRAVELLING SECOND CLASS THROUGH HOPE

Embarrassed like the moon at midday

I set my watch 30 minutes fast this morning
and watched myself sleep a while

touching the edges of the universe
others existing only in dreams

I pulled back the curtains
and witnessed the world coping without me

All day
I caught the change in people as I entered their lives

Saw how differently they behaved before I arrived
It was as if I was watching them dressing

Tomorrow I'll set my watch back an hour to see how other edges
close in as I leave

See myself as ghost in other dreams

Sans pretension

We say 'cul-de-sac'
to make 'dead end' sound sunny
We say 'nouveau riche'
instead of working class with money

We call art 'avant-garde'
when we don't understand it
Jumble sales sell 'bric-à-brac'
which must be French for shit

Let's call a spud a spud
no more lies or elaborate word contortions
Chips are chips
not pommes frites or french fries
Why say 'haute cuisine' when you mean 'smaller portions'

No more saying we had a 'tête-à-tête'
when you mean you've been nagging
bragging or just chin wagging

And no more calling it a 'ménage à trois'
when you mean three people shagging

The first time I died I was completely hopeless at it

There's St Peter at the gates of Heaven
doesn't know whether to close early for lunch
or hurry me up

God's scratching his head
The Devil's re-checking his inventory

Yes... no...?
People dying about me right left and centre
not giving it a second thought

There's me – more trouble than I'm worth
Dithering
Stuck in some universal revolving door
waving my arms about, trying to attract attention

Am I early?
Er... Shall I come back later?
Er... Is there a queue? Er...

Some cherubim start to put down their harps
and come to see what all the fuss is about

Others play louder hoping I'll go away

Past relatives, realising it's me, skulk off
into a blinding light

The Devil starts looking concerned
and sneaks out a bottle of Tippex

Sitting on the idea of grass

Sitting on grass
worms writhe in wet soil only a breath beneath the surface
insects inch between blades

This is not the idea of grass
upon which you're sitting

of village cricket and croquet on the lawn
of parasols and summer picnics
of green carpets and rose gardens

Eating cheese
it is not the view through the microscope you are eating

Admiring a body
it is not the tissue and fibres, the bones and the organs you
hold in mind

Falling in love
you select your level of perception

She loves me, she loves me not

Eternity comes and goes as easy as that
like the crossing of the equator
or the passing of infection
there is something, then there is nothing
and somewhere in-between
there is change

Blood rushes from the heart to the head
and back to the heart
once, twice
and somewhere on its return
or its migration out again
there is change

Breath enters the lungs and
is expelled
once, twice
and somewhere between the expulsion
and the intake of fresh air
there is change

Sensation excites the nerves
the pupils dilate and retract
pores react to temperature
yet even without perceived movement
time passes
there is change

Images illustrate the mind
some erratic, some fluid
conscious and subconscious
some casual, some revealing deliberation
the world outside is as yet unaltered but
there is change

The Dinosaur War poems

65 million years BC – February 3rd – Thursday

To Hell with the lot of them, that's what I say.
This ice age is no place for a poet.
Fight and eat, eat and fight, that's all they know.
It's like talking to an amoeba.
"We need to evolve," I told them.
"We need a thumb."
"Warm blood," I said. "That's the future."
But all they do is stomp around trying to look frightening.
Nothing much happening. Went to bed early.

65 million years BC – February 4th – Friday

"OK let's invent fire," I said.
No response.
"What about the wheel?"
Nothing.
We foraged around for leaves for a while.
Alan tried to charge a tree.
There was nothing we could do for him.

65 million years BC – February 5th – Saturday

A stegosaurus next to me in the mud is bleeding.
He's resting between bouts with a pterodactyl.
I explained to him about air superiority.
Suggested we improve our ground-to-air technology.
He tried to gouge me with his horn.
I've got a bad feeling we're not going to make it.

65 million years BC – February 6th – Sunday

There's fierce fighting near the ravine.
No-one seems to have noticed the ice is receding.

I don't like the look of the dust that's
blowing in from the south.
Everyone's moving out.
I showed the General my plans for an 'eco-dome'
which I believe could maintain and perpetuate a friendly
environment indefinitely.
He ate them.

65 million years BC – February 7th – Monday

This morning we came across a herd of creatures
we had never seen before. All of them were dead.
A couple of the older tyrannosaurs wanted to turn back.
Fires are burning all around us now.
It's hard to tell the difference between night and day.
I can't believe there is still fighting.
The only thing that pulls me through is I know in my heart
God is on our side.

65 million years BC – February 8th – Tuesday

I woke up sweating. No idea of the time.
I tried to find out as I have a feeling these little details
are important somehow.
Anyway the point is I'd been dreaming.
Well it was more of a nightmare really.
All I can remember was that I was dead
and someone or something had re-assembled my bones
but had gotten it wrong.
I tried to correct them, diplomatically at first, but they
assured me they knew more about it than I did.
We began to fight. That's when I woke up.
I'm not sure of the time. It was late, I know that.

Lying about your age

Against nature you choose to stunt progression

Devaluing yourself
betraying new friends
you dishonour cherished moments
and demean suffering for mathematics

Instant time travel within a vacuum
you lose faith
misalign the stars
and redraw the truth as misfit

Never play chess with an anarcho-nihilist

I tried to play chess with an anarcho-nihilist once
Every move I made he questioned

He continually changed the rules
but later claimed that there weren't really any in the first place

He said "Any piece can go to any position on the board it wants
when it wants"

He kept making three or four moves at a time
Then when it suited him he moved my pieces out of the way
Sometimes into other rooms

He refused to place any of the pieces centrally in the proper squares
He declared such divisions to be 'false borders'
and started painting out the white squares at random

When I announced it was check mate and that I'd won
he just kicked the table over and
flushed my king down the loo

Life after forever

It's always harder for the gardener
to smell how sweet the flowers are
with the stench of manure still on his palms

From the first warm blood in the water
nature has never invested in failure
A call for moral justice would have us all shot at dawn

There's more courage in the hand that re-enters the flame
than in all the arrogance of those yet to fail

Your room

You're painting your nails
in your bedsit coffin
cleaning your mug whilst still drinking your coffee

eating sleeping drinking and waiting
as the tears dry you're there repainting

cleaning up the dust the Hoover missed
never allowing anything to rust
nothing must, not in your room

You're changing the cover and matching pillows
painting out mirrors
and painting out windows in your room

Between brush strokes you're hesitating
I know you're in there
I can hear you painting

A baby magpie

Yet only a few days old
in moments of solitude that follow
does this life even now herald
a little sorrow

Concerning loss and theft

I've lost something valuable or had it stolen
So I'm forced to retrace my mundane actions
these tiny harbingers whose whispers
now mock with megaphones

The margin of error
I've recently allowed myself
widens from the gap at back of a settee
to the Grand Canyon

Re-assessing even the most casual of contact
my mistrust embitters charity
I've become Machiavelli dusting for prints
undermining all integrity in trial by memory

No matter whether it turns up
or not
I feel I've lost something valuable
or had it stolen

There will come a time you will no longer set aside one day a week for tears

your heart seems hesitant between each beat
and serenity is never so easily charted
not even on the most detailed atlas

for there appears an honesty
within your quiet breathing
to which these sad poems aspire

it is time, perhaps
to set aside a little compassion
and to court yourself

Heavy Goods Vehicle

hugging
the
inside
lane

a giant
morse
code

we
own
the
dark
road
home

stamina
not
speed
now
virtue

a slow
cure
along
the
back
bone

sleep
walking
beyond
the
cathode

pilgrims
and
heroes

Stealing the scream

Poetry reduced to the metric
the shrill too raw for comfort, the anguish untidy
The pitch not conducive to the cosy aesthetic
Sport replaces anarchy

Concealed and congealed in the mud mundane
defined and refined in reason
The sum of mass and energy remains
yet something divine is missing

In a world without scrapes, Pluto remote
my shadow cast in outline only
I have been rendered sedate, the wrong ghost
there is no desperation to pierce me

Skeleton

My teeth are somewhat corroded by sugar
but otherwise despite my figure
my skeleton is not dissimilar to yours

My muscles are weak and wasted
and through lack of use have degenerated
but these will rot long before my bones

My stomach and my legs are swollen
my neck and jowls have become misshapen
All this will disappear as we grow nearer

The soothing of elasticity has deserted my face
my eyes have lost focus with age
soon my hair will begin to skulk away

There is a scent and a texture to my skin
that has at times been found attractive
This will quickly lose its lustre

Personality is demonstrated with each single move
from grace to tragic ineptitude
but inanimate, history will spar with others

Through my conscious fears and aspirations
I unfold my dreams and passions
though with the failing of light my body will fall derelict

And in a thousand years' time
outlasting it all
in a museum or some lecture hall

the scaffold of my core
may well hang side by side with yours
with labels almost identical

There is no need for the family to huddle round the fire

The focus of the living room is switched to the TV
It sheds a different light
at the touch of a button, at the turn of a dial

instant lukewarmth
No-one stares for hours into the heart of a radiator
No-one basks in the glow of underfloor heating

the temperature is maintained uniform throughout
no mess, no inconvenience
like an acquaintance, a lodger, a flat mate

In years to come will Guy Fawkes be sat
on a huge air conditioning unit
whilst we watch fireworks via broadband?

Welcome to the City of Self

The above phrase was found graffitied on Edinburgh Art Gallery during the Fringe in 1990

Welcome to the City of Self
where the body of Christ becomes bread and jam
The beast with a thousand I's
I leaflet therefore I am

Winning boat races tie at Oxbridge
careerists frigging in the rigging
It's the death of a sales pitch
where the one line quote is king

Where it takes 200 to tango
Fast talking at the running buffet
Is there a medical student in the house
or is everyone's name really 'lovey'?

Beauty hangs its head
where the commonplace has no worth
where once the touch of another's hand
might have been the greatest show on Earth

There's an old man dead in the gutter
there are razor blades stained by a bath
but in the carnival nothing else matters
except he who gets the last laugh

Tuning up with the 'me me me'
the sell-by-date of the year
If Van Gogh had had to play Edinburgh
he'd have cut off his other ear

Chapel of the Metal Shroud

I stand before you as faith
in accuracy and a system man-made

in distance and the white line
in direction and the painted sign

in measurement and ordained barriers
in technology and the road builders

in evolution and the mechanic's skill
in instinct and the common will

in order over the unknown
in yourself and those close to

in the motives of strangers
in society and human behaviour

Purity of spirit comes in all waist sizes

Patronised as character
the problem is not glandular
The problem is only the perception of glamour
a perfect anatomy provides no real armour

There is no correlation between girth and worth
we play the glands we're dealt at birth
Lift up your chins, live fat die full
build your bonfires on the highest of hills

Physical presence is but a folly
only the depth of the soul is measured as holy
Angels are never spotty, hunchback, nor bald
bone structure is transparent in the weighing of souls

The reflection in the back of God's spoon

Nude modelling for the afterlife
she secures the burger concession in Paradise

It's difficult to be concerned at the world's wrongs
with an industrial base of cream scones

There are dead moths at your altar
Theme parks replacing the landscapes of human nature

There's an empty funhouse with a Formica carousel
A gardener nurturing humanity on the high road to Hell

Originality for the mass market reaped with a vengeance
Individually wrapped tears and brutal indifference

As reproach stalks this poetry in thin disguise
for dogs bound by pavement there is little pride

All the seas of mercy yet to understand
I feel the sadness of computers in an enchanted land

How can the mortician fill dead bodies with formaldehyde
then go home and make love to his wife?

The wasting of limbs and the squandering of belief
Perpetual emotion and the dignity of trees

It's fear of death beating the wings of my heart
I reach for your hand in the dark

I reach for your hand in the dark

Ten ways to end a relationship

After Adrian Mitchell

1. *PATRIOTIC*
   I've got to dedicate myself to work of national importance

2. *SNOBBISH*
   Your time allocation has expired

3. *OVERWEENING*
   You are too fine a human to be held back by constraints

4. *PIOUS*
   I shall pray you find happiness elsewhere

5. *MELODRAMATIC*
   I'll kill myself rather than go through this torture any longer

6. *PATHETIC*
   I'm not worthy of love – I can't stand anyone to see me like this

7. *DEFENSIVE*
   I don't have to give reasons

8. *SINISTER*
   I've been sleepwalking with a bread knife lately

9. *LECHEROUS*
   I want to fuck your best friend

10. *PHILOSOPHICAL*
    Well were we really going out anyway?

There's always room in the hearse on the way back

Joseph plays the percentages
he can be eyeing up four women in different parts of
the same room

He takes his data day diary literally
A wall chart of his sperm level would read like a cardiac arrest
To him love is a dog with six legs

Relationships, just things that crash in the night
Loyalty, a free fall from infatuation to indifference
from the erotic to the erratic

There is a need to prove that he can still compete

To Joseph
nature gives no time to niceties
forever, comes with in-built obsolescence

There always appears a point in coupling when he feels like
he's stuck next to someone on a long coach journey having ran
out of conversation

In despair, it is of course the things we don't say that shout
the loudest
Joseph mutilates his every hour

I don't believe he chooses to be ugly
it is merely an ailment
a sickness of the spirit

Joseph's crime is that of cowardice
He has spent his whole life running with the eye of the storm
and destiny seems such a big word for such a small return

Cranking up suspense in adolescence
the pivot and swerve, the running of the escalator
carnal desire his internationalle
Joseph shies away from the need of a meaning

For the ultimate taboo is to be lonely even for a second
and so to fail, to be an object of pity, to be a loser
and clichés become clichés for a reason
no-one, but no-one, loves a loser

It is to strands of this he ties his final submission

hoping as mortality yawns
hoping as the sediment thaws
hoping as the essence pulls immediate to his breath
that his lies are lies after all

All kids are born with long thin moustaches

Like most kids I suppose I was a natural surrealist
I used to think nothing of playing football for hours
in my cowboy outfit

I had no concept of relative scale
and no distinct understanding of the comparative relationship
between any two objects

My Action Man would regularly hitch lifts
straddled across a 2-inch Matchbox fire engine

Toilet rolls, shoeboxes, Elastoplast reels,
coat hangers and Fairy Liquid bottles
were all stock multi-faceted components
to fit into any imaginary playworld

But never
and I always felt this to be one of the major drawbacks to my creativity
the double-sided sticky tape *Blue Peter* and *Magpie* presenters
somehow always assumed you'd have lying around
For years I pictured all middle-class kids having drawers full of the stuff

Large cardboard boxes could change in seconds
from racing cars to jet planes or speed boats
just by a slight alteration in the accompanying engine noise
Any sheet or tablecloth became a tent which I'd just sit in for days
and days and days

One of my very favourite games
was when the British 8th Army desert patrol Airfix soldiers
would fight off the alien spaceship
which was always made out of Lego
and manned by Fuzzy-Felt farm animals

Travelling second class through Hope

With softer spine you rise and shine
and strap yourself safe in time

More beads for the natives, more gongs for the troops
you buy off the kids with spaghetti hoops
melt into the monotone, the drip-feed TV
Death Wish 4, Funland UK, until you say

Is   this   all   there   is   ?

You say you need a cause, you need to fight
you're looking for something, anything
If only you had something noble denied
sometimes you say you'd fight everything

So down at the beast market
you seek solace in your crisps
Hey, what's a nice Jaeger jumper like that
doing in a place like this?

You see Madonna singing 'Material Girl'
to earthquake victims in The Third World

You see a white car drive through Soweto
swords designed as shields
the new credit card diplomacy
and the worship of God on wheels, and you say

Is   this   all   there   is   ?

And when the party's over, and limp lettuce and lager trodden into the carpet are no longer part of the fun. And you realise that the Earth doesn't revolve around three pubs in the centre of town. And you realise your God's not bigger than my God after all. Travelling second class through Hope, you pray, there must be more than this.

Cornerhouse

Permanently at a crossroads
I glory in my window seat
The goldfish outside
don't realise the irony of the screenplay for
today I am Richard Basehart
Schools of buses
migrate towards Piccadilly Gardens
as I chart a course for the rest of my life
People with bigger fish to fry
circle the glass
their faces mouthing in silence

Yesterday I was mistaken for Bergman
in Panoramic Cinemascope
austere against a backdrop of grey and white
but no... I was on top of a bus
front seat
bound for Skegness

Then 2000 years later that afternoon
on the bridge of the Enterprise
I was left in control of the console
the red alert button
resembling a buttered scone
screen on
Spock dead
my ship infested with aliens
my finger poised over a protruding sultana

But today
my body feels as heavy as a shipwreck
I am safe in the deep of my third cuppa
periscope down
listening for sonar
avoiding the sharks and the mermaids

Pragmatic romanticism

1. ...for want of a better word we call it love

With your leg bent over mine I can feel the moistness of your desire
With your breast cupped against my lifeline I can feel the flourish
       of your heart
There is a dance within your pulse

2. Some days I lie in bed all morning waiting for the phone to ring

I could get up but I need outside intervention
some stimulus, catalyst, impetus
the doorbell to buzz, the landlord to knock,
the window cleaner to bruise his ladders against the paintwork
a poster to fall from the wall, the bedroom to burst into flames
anything

I am already dead
my carcass exhumed to imitate devotion
Some days I close my eyes
and take my heart off the hook

3. Though the world now lies empty as the dialogue in a cheap
       porn movie

once, maybe
on another continent
where the sky seemed wider
allowing arms to stretch out and loosen the joints

If there is no such thing as true love then all logic is built
on the smallest unit of time

Only Christmas and birthdays bring death this close

Overnight you have grown old
and though spite is no spur to succeed
in the absence of caress it can suffice

Only yesterday
with hair dye and vitamins
you boasted you had cheated time
but now it is the last dance of the party and
the prospect of a taxi home alone
rises like a flush within your cheeks

Years you wasted
slip through the doorway
giggling together adolescent
clear skin and eyes so bright
and always with partners that look such fools
but young

It is not them you hate but their youth
There is no individuality in this attraction merely the
aesthetics of innocence
and you, clinging to that one chance
force yourself into the night air before
the indignity of being the last to leave

I have seen you in the morning
lost in some mundane task
unaware of my presence
There is a subtlety of emotion that wisps around your eyes
You hesitate behind each door
What worries you most is the loss of appetite

Where once you were so sure
diplomatic farewells have beaten back your pride

Where once you were curious
the nakedness of longing has sought to scar your faith
breathe still
no whim of nature will chill your soul tonight

there are traditions that carry the truth of seasons
there are books that will outlast technology
we are old friends you and I
rest your fears against these words
it'll be alright
it will be alright

The 44th minute

All I want now is
to be in wonder
immersed

Reminded purity exists
somewhere
in this universe

New friends tell me I've become disfigured in repartee

that all softness or aggression is passé
that detachment is sophistication
To think it should come to this
Your eyes were emerald
and there was a simple joy
in watching you brush your hair

As if bewitched by childhood I have seen you dazzle
I have lightened my frown to the bond of sweethearts
I have chanced the whirlwind of derision
and as enchantment ends
on yet another carriage I cower from
Chinese whispers that taunt floodlights on my illusions

Sometimes I wonder if I've ever been in love
it's like trying to explain why a joke is funny

No matter how I feign indifference I still fear flying
As each plane leaves the ground my prayers are of you
If the soul survives I want above all to hold your presence
This may not weigh heavy in the glib torrent of conversation
but at times such as these those moribund do not lie
not to themselves

I realise to you I am already fable
It seems I lost you even before we met
Don't look at me now
I've grown old and ugly
whilst you remain
breathless as a new constellation

February

Least favoured of the dozen

She does not promote sales like January
to some the first disappointment of the calendar

She does not offer optimism or resolve with the
freshness of a truly clean sheet

She does not promise new life
with the same authority as her replacement

She is never sure how she should be clothed
the best winter costumes already modelled

The spring collection held back
there is a feeling of making up the numbers

February is a corridor of a month
Leap year she smiles that extra smile

but it is the fleeting smile of a receptionist
or a cloakroom attendant

A more intimate fame

She licked the applause from the fingers of each hand
like honey drips from toast
but could never hold on tight enough
to that for which she hungered most

Only let into the heart like a holiday home
though always a paying guest
Scratching for dignity from blind hope
but knowing dignity is still second best

Love has always been one of those rooms at parties
that she'd never dare venture inside
where close friends sat cross-legged on floorboards
and she had no invite

Always outstretched arms at railway stations
into which she'd never run
or couples on buses in matching jumpers
unashamed to dress as one

This time though she thought she'd sneaked unnoticed
into the gates of Heaven accepted for her sins
but she clung too tight never understanding
how fragile a thing are wings

and when the regret welled up inside
there was no cradle for her soul and her broken pride
How can it hurt so much if the love has died?

and soon all the narrow eyes and shallow lives
became a noose around her neck
until accelerating into fog the drink cocooned her head
how can you love so much and have nothing left?

Within your arms

If you were
        water
I would laze in your caress
and if you were fire
I would bathe in your passion

If you were air
I would breathe in your perfume
and if
       you were wool
I would wrap myself in your warmth

and
if you were
       darkness
I would lose myself in you
               forever

Why you never look like Paul Newman on family photos

Snapshots snag real life
full of misdirected angles

blurred vision
faces disappearing off edges

people betrayed by their expression
likenesses half caught

shadows masking the image
outlines cluttered and confused

poses thrown by the unexpected
objects obstructing the foreground

strangers intruding into the background
characters unready or self-conscious

identities distorted by perspective
detail erased by exposure

features too close to register but more often too far away
figures dwarfed by a vast expanse of sky

The third person

Using they instead of I
they generalize
and rationalise to anaesthetise

from the emote to the remote
in the they and the he
in the they and the she

They no longer enjoy they appreciate
They no longer experience they spectate

bureaucrats of passion
they no longer feel but relate
they no longer talk but discuss
they no longer argue but debate
they no longer react but equate

They dilute to nullify
from the nib to the cursor
as they distance themselves
in the third person

Dopey and Juliet

We are watching a new adaptation of *Romeo and Juliet* but
it is ridiculous to empathise with the leading characters

Mawkish fascination has laid waste to my valour
and my body creaks like a faulty windscreen wiper

I can no longer read the nakedness of your face
How I react is no reflection on you
How you react is not necessarily a reflection on me

Your eyes remain unchanged but
you wear the years apart like a new fashion

I'm sure the main actors mock my tentative appearance in this scene
I would feel easier if this were *Beauty and the Beast*
or more comfortable even with the part of Dopey in *Snow White*

You touch my hand and reassure me that we can be friends now
I'm certain in your version I'm not even in this play

I have taken on the role of an old work colleague that it's
nice to see for two minutes but could become tiresome over the
course of a few drinks

Your elbow is close but you can't bite it

Now smarts like laughter in the art gallery
like the piercing of a balloon
like the panic mid-fall

A revelation too commonplace
any bride's father
awaiting the wedding car could explain

The past – some other lifetime away
paling intuition
growing on the back of now

The future – a scaffold to infinity
possible now to be relished
promises of now in which to excel

A conscious now holds my hand
deliberate amid a most solid universe
now so loud Cupid would need ear defenders

I am sitting with you again

As usual you are courting solitude
You are browsing possible lifestyles
and though I am troubled by the vivid contrast
I will not discolour this silence

Lost within your glossy magazine
colour co-ordinated rooms do not allow
for the frailty of the hesitant
and the self-conscious

I will try to fake nonchalance when your eyes eventually
look up from the page
In the time it takes
for a breath to change from inward to outward
we are re-writing a new future

I am sitting with you again
You are somewhere
where the stars offer different possibilities
but there is no distance between us

Civic statues are never naked

Proud for posterity
Jaw set
Self-aware
Inactive
Like a solid photograph
This is the official face
Formal dress
Dignity without vulnerability
A permanent 'Sunday best'
Grandeur selected to inspire
Without tenderness
Sterner than life
Humanity reduced
for the importance of stonework

In the open court of mountains like 12 angry jurors

Hypnotized by oncoming headlights
the idiot beguiled
with humour as bleak as a highland loch
mocked with accommodating smiles

Still looking for love as hardy as bluebells
betrayal's quite funny really
we hide emotions behind glass
never seeing too clearly

Infatuation's a sight common enough
a love-lost caricature
just another walk on part
with delusions of grandeur
who would kiss your blood
and believe it pure

Eternal promises are for All Fools' Day
comically cruel
so mist now softens the skyline
whilst I band aid the ridicule

In the open court of mountains like 12 angry jurors
I serve my solitude
I feel no guilt, though I know I shouldn't
I miss you

Time passed unnoticed until she took the clock

Slumped on your chair like dead weight at an orgy
coughing like an S-reg Fiat
though you've lit up a thousand churches in prayer
you know she's not coming back

Overfat on time
you say "age doesn't matter" then you lie about your own
if you live to be 100 you'd still be afraid of dying too young
switching off the bedside lamp shadows crowd the void
but the patterns on the wallpaper don't scare you anymore
it's the blank spaces now that threaten
Nothing, not even love, survives within a vacuum

Fast approaching your love-by date
you count the days left unkissed
Age
has become just another stick to beat yourself with

Where once your passion was an elevator between Heaven and Hell
Where once you believed love dripped from between her legs

There in the absence of children
sex grew tired on easy living
becoming a parasite on the back of routine
and all the words you chose so carefully
blew like so much litter
Conversations became quieter
and as scarce as in a spaghetti western
Laughter became a missing person

until
you couldn't remember kissing her face when you last made love
and her lips became just hooks to hang your heart upon

and though you look for that face from the window of every train
the photo in your pocket is now starting to fade
and though you curse the new diary with each year that arrives
you never noticed the clock on the wall until it kissed you goodbye
you never noticed the clock on the wall until it kissed you goodbye

Learning to understand the mechanics of the eclipse

Only the youngest of women left their scent
and friends thought this an inadequacy
Whilst to Nick, as he would have you believe
it was between himself and God alone

Licking the thighs of other women
in the naked sighs of other women
Nick blurred into all humanity

In the schedules of other women he sipped tea
In the flurry of sweat and breath he fought to contain the clouds
Whether he tripped, or was pushed, or whether he jumped
he glimpsed weakness, once and forever weakness

Pressed to the nipple of other women
he crowded his floors
with the tissue bodies of liquid promises
and the scattered mourning clothes of bloodrush and desire

Until, between the devil and the deep blue eyes
grief like a panther fell on him
but here now curled up in his arms
the crying wound of another's penance

Nick had become a bit player in another's nostalgia
Between empty sheets
token gifts winced at the coldness of dead flesh
Here, the softest of mirrors

and now, time to discover
just how pure the bottom line
just how myopic the personification of love
just how selfish melancholy

The accidental death of a cat

Outside the polling office
I saw a cat that had never voted
run over by a man-made machine
that failed to notice

Like a circus crowd
a random cross-section of the electorate
spectated, as spasms of pain
jerked the body into acrobatics

Someone went to phone
but to phone who?
Someone went to find the owner
Someone went for a half-brick

the cat lay still at last, one eye dangling loose
like a battered old teddy bear
The half brick was discarded
The cat placed reverently into a Safeway's carrier bag

The crowd dispersed
The afternoon sun dried
the small smudges of blood
into the tarmac

The colours meshed so that soon you
could hardly notice the difference
when you passed
Later than night all parties claimed victory

No game show will ever hold your worth

I noticed on your windowsill
two broken flowers in a small glass
These were not set in pride of place but lay unassuming
like children huddled in the dark

Their stems too short now to fit the vase
convenience would have them dumped in a bin liner
but something in you
could not let even this
seemingly dispensable
frail beauty die

I know such an action is no great gesture but only a tiny
moment in a far corner of the rush
but it is a victory
an everyday victory
and its colour should flutter within each heart

You, who are capable of such casual tenderness
what worlds your palms could describe
no game show will ever hold your worth
no computer ever measure your soul

whilst there is the merest glimmer of humanity
we are none of us lost

we are not lost

A farce is still a farce even with subtitles

and she tells me she loves him
with her hand stroking my inner thigh
Her face is symmetrical and her sweat has a pleasant composition
We are exchanging pretty lies like cigarette cards

Stifling disinterest like two old soldiers between battles
The mutual gratification of animal lust seems a distinct possibility
We are both whores to romance
but it is all too predictable

There is no pilgrimage in her fingertips
only the musing of calculation
and I wonder if my face displays its weariness
An idle stubble scratches the sheen from her make up

There is no nourishment in these overtures
only the mechanics of anatomy, a series of shrugs
How can your blood race so fast
but your heart remain unmoved

I don't have to wait for the morning to hate myself
Pitiful and pathetic seem insults too well used to scald disgust

When I look into the mirror, if I concentrate on the centre
features of my face, I can see how I used to look in my teens
Is it guilt that's swollen my neck
or my face wrapping itself against the world?

The desire to wipe the slate clean, to start a new jotter
competes each day against the easier option to drown all vivid
images in maudlin and lie, before God's feet, face down in the subway
stained with my own piss

As you can see I try my best to romanticise this predicament
but tacky affairs always remind me of cheap early seventies movies

I turn my back when we've made love

I turn my back when we've made love
but not turned against you
My thoughts are of you
the curve of your body marks the horizon
the scent of you I cherish along my skin
Memories of our sex perfumes distant vales
blood has not yet settled

I've slept this way since childhood
through marriage and a dozen affairs
Unfortunately there are some things you can't unlearn
In sleep as in spirit we fall alone
though I long to drift in endless embrace
though open mouthed I wish for the cliché of souls entwined
this is the folly of gift shops

I will always sleep apart
Lie close
and still
we are tired as only lovers can be

Love – the disaster movie

she said she hated you / loathed you / found you utterly repulsive / but you tried not to take it personally / now you're standing in an empty room making a cup of tea you don't want / and being over-nice to people you hate / measuring your success by counting the things you'll never have / you turn on the tv to watch black and white nothing / for a few pounds more you could have coloured nothing / you go to the pessimists' club twice a week now, it gives you something to look forward to / you used to worry about your lack of troubles / lying in the sun praying you didn't get skin cancer / now you're trying to capture the world in one sentence / dressed as lamb, you beef about the price of love / dressed to kill you sacrifice yourself / standing in your perfect world you look out of place / oh the words you almost said may make you great someday / if only you knew the rules you'd ignore them / you shrug your shoulders, some you lose… and some you lose / there's plenty more fish in the sea you said, but now diving in you feel like a fish out of water and look for corners in the goldfish bowl / people tell you to be yourself but that's not like you / when you're not thinking of her / you're thinking of thinking of her / you see yourself as a prisoner trapped in a world of reason / whose crime is that of wanting her / whose sentence is that of loving her / and whose only escape is to her / you're living in a world of aliens / you feel like the skeleton in your own cupboard / like someone's playing loud music at your funeral / it's no fun being depressed you complain / with the ultimate vanity you believe your inferiority complex is of a superior nature / you believe some people wouldn't recognise love if you beat them to a pulp with it / what did she mean we've got nothing in common? you say / it's her, I've got plenty in common / you wonder whether you'd rather be loved / or love someone / or be in love with someone you love and who loves you / and realise you don't ask for much / you used to be lovers / now you're just good friends / that means she ignores you as though an embarrassment / and you watch your words when you meet unexpectedly / I used to be sensitive you explain / but I'm alright now, do you think?

Someone tossed a match into the corner of our past

Someone tossed a match into a corner of our past
It was the darkest corner
where rubbish had collected unseen

Out of curiosity
I kindled the flame
By its flicker I could gradually recognise
each item of debris

Sickened with fascination
I nurtured the fervour until it blazed with fury
casting shadows onto the rest of our lives

It raged with self-destruction
It raged with despair
Everything and anything it could
it would drag down and wound

Until
wounded itself, blind and dying
strangled by its own appetite
it shrunk and curled

I leave the ashes now as a reminder
I ought really to clear them away
They seem so small reduced to cinder

It's childish I know but
the heat has scorched so much
I have to show you before they're
finally swept

Demoting Cupid to a chat show host

I'm having to be polite
with someone whose nipples I licked
less than seven days since
Someone whose craving
hung so vulnerable on my fingertips

It's a strange courage
that sees flight as dignity
She is talking to me now in the language of social workers
offering fragments of explanation
like corners from some complicated jigsaw

Waving at the window
as if to wipe an image from the glass
When a child falls
there's a moment when
it doesn't know whether to laugh or cry

It seems at the narrowest junctions
my future sits before me
purposely waiting for the lights to change
then indicates
against the oncoming traffic

Hell is a place where all the photos you thought you'd safely destroyed are enlarged

Yesterday
all the litter that I'd thrown away throughout my life
came round to visit me

It demanded to be let in
said we needed to talk

Feeling guilty at the ease with which I'd so conveniently discarded it
I let it in
There hardly seemed room for it all

The used tea bags alone filled the kitchen
and there were margarine tubs and toenail clippings
I hadn't seen for ten years or more

Strange now to think
how they used to be very much part of my life at one time
I confess I found it difficult to relate

I've changed a lot
I'm sure some of the litter has changed
It's bound to have
The half-used tin of tomatoes from April 1964 certainly had

A chipped mug with no handle took the initiative
it asked why I never rang
"I kept meaning to" I lied, "but I've lost the number"

The number itself
cowered on a screwed-up piece of paper and said nothing

Sharing the same piece of paper
the words 'I'm sure we can still be good friends'
blushed like felt tip

Several old shoes, a left-handed glove
a recent batch of razor blades and numerous bread wrappers
each with one crust left in
began to edge round the topic of coming back

The remains of an Airwick Solid opened up trying
to clear the air

The atmosphere was getting a little uncomfortable
A few old fly papers conceded
that they had never really held out much hope
and had only come along with the rest

There was an awkward silence
when I introduced the new bin bags

Eventually I managed to persuade
all but one or two piccalilli jars
that coming back maybe wasn't such a good idea

and after a few hours
we parted amicably enough

I don't think there'll be any further visits
for a while at least

even so
I don't know that I like the way
the swing bin now looks at me
knowingly

King Street

I once set myself adrift at a jumble sale
watching pregnant craving in frenzy

And I have no wish to pretend I am in London
I have no desire to be at the centre of things

When I couldn't afford to buy
these windows intimidated

Today they are like Christmas trimmings
left up too long

Once I turn the corner onto Cross Street
I am back in Manchester

The ratio of stone to glass
suggesting a reflection of substance

Mixed metaphors

Upon recognition, an outburst of enthusiasm and then
we'd probably struggle to find something in common

Old friends seeking points of reference
as awkward as mixed metaphors

with words like anti-climax and disappointment lurking in the wings
but even so, I'd still like us to meet up again someday

ideally in passing, when rushing for a train
with just enough time to test the water

sketch in the bare bones of a future conversation
and most importantly, in case we never meet again

to say those simple but difficult things we should, but never do, say
consoling ourselves with phrases like "can't be put into words"

Those most important of things never said but
just drowned in the moment and lost in the shuffle

Tomorrow's worms (a love poem to critics)

Born
 without
  backbones
   they ooze
   from their
    holes
     they are
    processors
    of sewage
     a linear
      arse machine
       two-faced
        they digest
         and excrete
          they're
           proof
          you are
          what you eat
         a cannibal
         realisation
         of reincar-
          nation
          experts
          deem them
          necessary
           for more
           than just
            easy quarry
            bad weather
             brings them
              to the
               surface
               if you
               cut them
               in two
               do it
               length
               ways

Recoiling from the anti-climax

I have seen disappointment
in eyes like undertakers
sizing up my future

in limp handshakes
and blank glances at wristwatches
in the tactical retreat to the toilet

in forced smiles
and edgy non-specific answers
in the shifting of focus

in conversations that talk around or over
sometimes even through
in the contortions of cocktail diplomacy

in the appointment remembered
in the sudden relapse
in the unexpected duty

in the body language of the dispassionate
in those with the ease to mingle
and as always

I am left with the awkwardness
knowing that any gesture I make
any fight any sacrifice

will be
a disappointment

Owning imperfection

We are the imperfect
the rejected
the bruised
the damaged goods
the misshapen fruit

the crop that failed to make the grade
the eggshell that couldn't take the strain
the discounted
the allowable waste
the below standard

the bottom of the range
the potatoes with too many eyes
the slow mover putrefied
the garment soiled
the bargain spoiled

the chipped and cracked
the squeezed and put back
the peas no longer tender and young
the incomplete
the thread undone

the scorned
the squashed
the marked
down
the grape unwashed

We are the imperfect
the rejected
the bruised
the aborted
the discontinued

Silence of the phone

The silence of the phone
is not just the silence of one person
but the silence of all humanity

Not only does she not want to speak to you
nobody wants to speak to you
not one person in the entire world

You are not only alone
but snubbed, ignored
rebuked by a conspired silence

A deliberate vindictive silence
not a pause or a shared silence
but a cold desolate silence

A silence
for which you are responsible
Your silence

There are many silences
the silence that passes between lovers unnoticed
the silence of a baby's sleep

the silence of a couple trapped in indifference
the silence of an empty chair
the silence before a suicide

and the silence of the phone
is the sum of all these
and more

When the time has come to leave

You can always tell when the time has come to leave
your things start to get put away in cupboards and drawers
out of sight

conversations quieten
people are busy when you enter a room
nobody looks you in the face or asks how you are

Mime doesn't pay

Last night I was burgled by a mime artist
He never made a sound

He could have got away with it
but then he tried to steal a piano I haven't got

He pushed and he pulled, he strained and he heaved
but it wouldn't move

Maybe, he thought, there was something valuable behind it
There wasn't

He tried to float the piano

He blew up a balloon and tied it to the piano
then he couldn't lift the balloon

I found him in the morning trapped inside an imaginary box

I called the police
He started to panic
tried climbing up a fictitious ladder

When the police arrived they let him out
He made a dash for it
tried running away on the spot

It took the police four hours to get him into the car
he kept getting pulled back by an invisible rope

I decided not to press charges
This afternoon I put an insurance claim in for the piano

Your favourite mug

Foolish I know
but I feel protective towards your favourite mug
I leave it around the house

as though you were still between sips
as if your lips were just out of the room a moment
and would soon enter and caress its brim

Alone at bedtime
I hold it gently, feel its warmth
and drink you in once more

Breaking up is …

Breaking up is…
making a conscious effort to say 'I' instead of 'we'
taking your number down from beside the phone

trying to play only records you never liked
pretending to be busy
trying to think of people worse off

mutual friends being diplomatic
saying 'at least you're both still young'
and 'at least you've got your health'

and other sentences all starting with 'at least'
planning the weekend around half a dozen eggs

not knowing what to do with hands
when walking down the street
finding people who look like you attractive

forgiving you everything
then nothing every other minute
discounting years in seconds

wanting to talk
but wishing too much hadn't been said already

Beyond mathematics

How much do I love thee?
Let me calculate the ways

Take the number of kisses
on the bottom of my letters
times
by the phone calls on your answering machine

Then add
warm bodies on winter nights
holding hands along the beach
and the moment you first thought of

Divide by
the forgotten anniversaries
the turning of a key in silence
and the emptiness of a meal for one

And what are you left with?

She has given herself

She has given herself
to the majesty of clouds discoloured
and the face of the moon dying in the west

She has given herself to the seasons
to the dreams of childhood
and to that which she can heal with her own hands

She has given herself to the storm from open sea
to the silence of a cold bed
and to the flight of the highest wing across the glare

If by chance she should see God
she would stare him full in the face
and would never be the first to look away

I'm talking to someone else's father

I was
I suppose
gay around the age of twelve and thirteen

Though to be honest
glandular activity being what it is
nothing was safe around that time

I'd have attempted sexual intercourse
with a tin of Swarfega
if that was the only way of achieving orgasm

It is quite common for lads
to become sexually aroused
climbing over furniture

It is not considered incitement
in these later years
to offer me a chair when I visit

When your eyes say 'I am here – is that not enough?'

James reaches out to grasp at something tangible
He counts the number of words in your compliment

He sets every affection into an overall picture
measures every gift against the past

If you tell him you love him he'll note it down
and consider it later

If you like a particular song he'll examine the words
for tell-tale signs of subconscious infidelity

If you cry he'll wonder if you're crying
for something he can't give you

In the happiest moments he steps back
and looks for approval

Even with eyes caught in a tender exchange
he feels lonely

He fears one morning when nothing in particular
seems to have happened
you'll come to him with your goodbye neatly folded
Even now your words haunt his pillow

Even now your words haunt his pillow

Happiness

    Happiness
           is relative
  a   distant   relative
the sort you see once a year
 and can never stop long

The lost generation of mermen and mermaids

I've flushed most of my descendants down the loo
unconsummated angels on clouds of tissue

I have squandered over five billion emissaries
en route to fertile ovaries

Wasted another five million destination unknown
stunting their growth much more than my own

Whole cemeteries of condoms I've created
non-starters not begat but now belated

The dumped diehard deliverers of DNA
trashed tadpole triggers of the family way

Minute Duncan Goodhews that got no further
than gossamer graves and milky mass murder

Cul-de-sac germination
timely entrapment and termination

A self-induced final solution
ethnic cleansing of my own evolution

Plain biscuits

Why do rich people insist it's
posh to eat plain biscuits

It seems to me Rich Tea are for the miserly
and Nice are not nice at any price
Shortbread I particularly dread
I'd sooner have a Happy Face instead

Tradition is fine for old codgers
but the young at heart want Jammy Dodgers
A plain Digestive is strictly for the restive
and not suggestive of anything festive

Similarly Garibaldis
are for the oldies
as only old fogies can be force-fed
a sandwich of bogies

Morning Coffee are easy to debunk
being impossible to dunk
An Arrowroot bicky
can also be tricky

Abbey Crunch or Bourbon Creams
are not the munch of my dreams
I'd sooner walk on hot coals bare foot
than eat Fig Rolls or Ginger Nut

and I'd sooner be aborted
than touch Teatime Assorted

yet I can eat Chocolate Hobnobs
no probs

A happy ending (revised)

…and they all lived happily ever after.

Well not all. Not all the time that is.

You've got to remember the book may have taken four or five hours to read but its story was meant to span several years. They obviously picked out the main action and discarded the mundane. You know, the trips to the toilet, the coming back to close the curtains, the days when someone wasn't feeling very clever so they just took it easy… that sort of stuff.

So when it says 'they all lived happily ever after' you have to take it as read there'd still be days, even weeks when nothing much happened. Someone might get a bit bored or feel a bit so so about an idea. Someone else might feel tired all of a sudden or feel that life was becoming repetitive, or passing them by.

The film was only an hour fifteen which meant they missed out a lot of the book. They even spiced up a few scenes to enhance the action.

So when it says 'they all lived happily ever after'
they meant that, on the whole, given the human condition
they had a relatively happy existence
remembering that they'd got over the worst of the bad stuff
during the making of the story,
forming as it did the basis of the plot
and given that we left the main characters on a high
as is the nature of romanticised story telling leading to such
an obviously flawed generalisation.

To Helena and back

There is no reasoning to your loneliness
You build your fireside on the most barren of landscapes
You offer your resignation from the vital

You are too concerned with structure and process

Those that wallow in reminiscence
suffocating all bitterness in nostalgia
deny the pain that the body needs
to summon the adrenaline
to heal the wound

But such observation is cerebral
even the sound of the vowels is the betrayal of compassion
It's actions not words that provide the most vivid memory

The gift I would bring to your christening
is courage in all things

Let the optimism you wear shame all contrived fashion

Unholy in the church of perfection
the stairs to forgiveness
are worn with the footsteps of those that falter

And you hold up your arms to the world
You wear desperation like a weight around your shoulders

There is no reason why I should save you

There is no reason why you should save me

Love like Hell

I have this theory that when you die your whole life is re-run like a sensorama video and you have to sit through it all again, every second, unedited, in a room with every friend and every relative that's been in the least bit involved. Now depending on what sort of life you've led this could be Heaven or it could be Hell. Think about it, everyone's going to see those private moments, those very private moments: farting in the bath; wiping bogies down the side of the armchair; every second of indulgent masturbation.

All the pathetic lies you told exposed for all to see; all the naff chat-up lines you used when you were a teenager, and still used later; all the places you had sex when you still lived at home. The things you did to get by; the way you justified it all to yourself and every really dumb-arsed no-balls shit-for-brains mistake you ever made you'll have to watch yourself make again.

But then
    maybe
        there'll be those moments of rare beauty; the moments of tenderness; the times you cried because you messed up; the things you meant to say; the questions in the mirror; the promises you made when you first held your own child; the nights you comforted another's despair; the time your lover's face glowed like beauty on fire; the times you said 'I love you' and believed your love would outlive the universe. The time you first held in your stomach thinking no-one would notice, and the regret in your eyes when you feared you were getting old. When you couldn't sleep one night and lay awake sweating and praying you didn't die before doing something, something, just something.

RAINING UPWARDS

"Do not be angry with the rain; it simply does not know how to fall upwards."
Vladimir Nabokov

The moon is leaving slowly

Every single star in the totality
pulls on my blood

Each individual atom
attracts

I am drifting
at the rate fingernails grow

If only
you could wrap your arms around me

Between neap and spring tides
as planets align
and the Earth slows

centrifugal force increasing
I am lifted

With zero the house always wins

Emptiness
is an even number
neither positive nor negative

Created in the imagination
as beautiful
a perfect circle

A hole
into which all the numbers in the universe
divide

Hard now to believe
there was a time
before quantification of that
which doesn't exist

uncontained
impossible to communicate
Only an unnamed absence

Who wasn't out to sea didn't pray to God

There is enough water here to drown every soul on Earth

We sit and watch white lines
break upon black slate

Trees and shrubs I can't name
claw at slopes whose classifications I can't pronounce

The whole facia falls bent and crumpled
like a broken roller coaster rail

These veterans
a wall-planner of existence

Humanity huddles at the inlets

Though we don't say as much
we share a cathedral sky with the distant clouds

the abandoned buildings
the quiet fisherman

the Easter sun
and the loneliness at the end of the ocean

Tunnelling into space

Why do we look for order and uniformity when

it is only though the unevenness
in the spread of hydrogen atoms
at the birth of the universe
that anything more exists

Through the patience of gravity on warps in space-time
through ultraviolet corrupting opaque clouds

through instability in generations of stars
through destruction and metamorphosis
on every scale

throuGh the random
and the chAos
the muTation and compliCation
the different
and the new

we arrive at that first connection within the womb
sparking
your
unique
brain
to life

The Second Punic War is not available on a tea towel

Fortifying lungs with calm
the first sight of snow for the
elephants from Carthage pulls
at the foothills of the Alps
now folded blue grey at dusk

Closing rays reach around peaks
clutch at clouds overcoming
mountains with long memories
one shadowing the other
ever into the distance

In the room of the hospice
we talk of anything else
Barbarians at the gates
Tectonic plates colliding
Invaders so far from home

The father of tactics sleeps
eventually humbled
bled by strategy unseen
We've learnt it is hard to change
direction within the charge

The toughest hide is fragile
I can but hope a plan will
form to delude my senses
as though one could charm cancer
as though Death himself would yield

As the ground accelerates towards you at an acute angle

If I tilt my head to the side
you are perpendicular
and the rest of this unholy mess
is at a slant

Italic trees in parallel
mark the degrees
ten past the hour

Dry leaves defy gravity
There is no slide to the east

Shadows brave the slope
The sun no longer certain
of its position

Toes grip for balance
Legs lengthen or shorten
to compensate

Fire engine red you stand out
amid the muted woodland

You lean against the sky like Atlas
carrying all on your back

"And wilt thou bend a listening ear to praises low as ours"
After Henry Kirke White

Where shadows are deeper shoulders fall
you can allow time for the aged and infirm

The hut of the old people
is given over to young bodies bolstered by rubber

Two fold-out chairs culture clash
amid abandoned clothing strewn on rocks

A flow of blood for heart and brain
excuse enough to bring your own stick to the beach

Three legs confuse the sand
Shuffle and tap lost to surf

Easing down on the front
well-ordered anarchy ensues

The ten-yard line ebbs and flows, fits and starts
reacts and breaks at its strongest point

We are relatively static
as the sun reflects on the outgoing tide

The world washed and scrubbed
fresh for a new adventure

All that learning and all that love
how can this not be a better day

Walking away is made up of several moments

Wanting to walk away

Seeing the possibility of walking away

Deciding to walk away

Turning and walking

Realising you are walking away

Deciding to keep walking

Knowing you are not going to turn back

Realising you are no longer walking away

Realising you are just walking

Not being afraid to look back

Not being afraid to look forward

Voice of the ancient babirusa

I am rendered immortal
my image digitally preserved
Ochre from the Ice Age
once immobile in this Sulawesi cave

The decay of uranium
confirms
over thirty thousand orbits
I have held my breath

From the right hemisphere of an early artist
I am born fully formed
This limestone you see behind me
this was our home

Now I will walk the world for him
Visit you
his descendants
in the place you call home

I have come to tell of a shared creativity
I have come to tell of an inner life
I have come to tell
he was not that different from you

A stream of consciousness meets the ocean

Like Rommel retreating from el Alamein
we are scattered across the sand

Waves clamber to reclaim the beach
leaving the man on his lounger as a pier

Another man patrols the shoreline
wearing a watch

The wind pelts my back with tiny meteors
acupuncture en masse

I take off my shoes
feel the grains on the flat of my feet

German dad in a mismatch of stripes
washes his kid's trunks in the swell

A cowgirl and Mrs Capone
model their new hats

There's a fat man in Speedos
like an egg in an egg cup

Striped awnings that offer a sliver of cover
contort in the breeze

as though invisible punkahwallahs
have gone apoplectic

Lovers enjoying their youthful bodies
trip themselves through the water

Teenage girls adjust bikinis
Yellow buoys bob like large bathtub toys

Mums slap suncream on infants' shoulders
like basting a roast

Ice lollies drip down sticks
Kids sit in holes the shape of cars and boats

Someone's asleep
with a towel over their head

A shanty town of windbreaks and umbrellas quiver
Futile mats instantly covered with sand

Young males show their prowess and agility
with two bats and a rubber ball

A small dog bounds from group to group
scaring the nervous

There's a disembodied head in the sea laughing
Abandoned dads build castles undeterred

A group of women stand at the water's edge
discussing sea temperature and the merits of immersion

The winner of the pinkest man of the year is revealed

A youth holds a rock the size of a skull
An impromptu Hamlet

then somewhere between shot put and discus
he hurls it into the sea

A boy carries a surfboard bigger than himself
A head, two feet and two hands float

A family re-enact the Olympic games
Long jump is easily mimicked

Surf boy tells his dad the story of his wave
his words crashing over each other

Too late a large woman in a thong bends down to stroke the dog
This could be any beach, any month, in any year

If it wasn't for a couple with a selfie stick
and the man with the e-cigarette

Nobody can remember who that is in the image

Is that me?
It doesn't look like me
I don't remember it being taken

It could be me
but what if I say it's me and it's not?
Am I living someone else's life?

Stealing someone's memories?
But then if it is me
who the hell am I?

I'm not this person am I?
I wasn't a moment ago
Now I'm this person and there's the proof

Have I been lying to myself all this time?
Do I have to make the decision?
Who am I to make that decision?

Fairy lights round a death bed

Tearing open the Christmas paper
it soon became apparent

Jutting out of the pillowslip
it had suggested itself at first glance

but disbelief had forced me
to re-appraise my suspicions

Now here it was confirmed
a ladder

Not a bright red ladder
Not a ladder adorned by Disney motifs

Just a plain ladder

The sort you might buy at any DIY store
I had not requested a ladder

The thought of receiving a ladder
had never crossed my mind

I had no more need for a ladder
than any other eleven-year-old

I checked to see if there'd been some mistake
but no, it was addressed to me

It was in my pillowcase
No-one claimed to know anything about it

There was no note or instructions
Ladders tend not to come with instructions

The remnants of a gymkhana

Closing my eyes in all this nature
seems a little churlish

It's the arse end of a farm
This ground is not designed for trainers

Man-made stuff sits scattered
like a junk yard

Candy-striped poles now caked in mud
lie like a kindergarten Waterloo

Traffic cones remain stubborn on sodden grass
Fallen leaves have outstayed their welcome

The rain dribs and drabs
like the last shakings of a drunk

The sky couldn't be more grey
Any British Standard colour chart would confirm

I can hear cars in the distance
Trains, helicopters even

In the field nothing moves
apart from the shimmering of poplars
forming a lofty chorus line

The gate is tinged green
like the wood is trying to re-root

This is not the rut I'm in
This is something different

Behind me a pale horse neighs
There's still hay to be had

Twigs and fences co-exist
Trees and timber
like life
living alongside the dead

Altruism

We are slicing up Albert Einstein's brain
like so much corned beef
dissecting the universe
behind those sad eyes

The guillotine falls with razor precision
the slivers are wafer thin
there is a finite amount of tissue

If we could
we would take a scalpel to his mind

He will never know of our results

We may discover no more than with any other brain

We may discover we are not deserving

Learning curves

The foetal position follows the curve of the lining
The placenta is circled to form a knot

The tongue is wrapped around the word 'mamma'
The sphere of the skull is soft

The child learns to judge the arc of the ball
The sun and moon mark day and night

A sail appears over the horizon
The outline of anatomy stimulates adrenalin

The foetal position follows the curve of the lining

An imaginary fly cannot be captured

After posh dessert in a paper dish
the debris of sugar scents the garden

This instant is an insect
Happiness the beat of a wing

A lazy summer evening recedes
at the pace of a picnic

Creation now sweetly attractive
our perception of time is a mismatch

Tea cups and beer glasses co-exist
as we share this flight of fancy

I appear to hold death in my hand
but mock gently as shadows stretch

You are intelligent and quick witted
Nothing will die today

in truth we both know
neither would harm the tiniest of souls

Though these human eyes are in need of focus
the joke we can see only too well

The shutter speed far too slow
timing is everything in comedy

Anticipation adds the necessary tension
It's there at your throat

Keep still, don't move
hold your breath

Anchor

There is something about a sense of scale
A small anchor is commonplace
almost a toy

But a real-size anchor
from a real-life ship
the sheer weight is impressive

Immovable
no tide or wind
can pull it away

Exhumed from the deep
it lies here
like a heart exposed

Sunglasses can make it seem darker than it actually is

We cast long shadows in the low sun
Though our shapes may be different
we are still connected

Outlines move across wet sand
and skirt rocks that reach for the surf
In this pause the elements are our playroom

We have made a companion of our solitude
I'm conscious of where my skin meets the air
how the pulse at the back of my neck softens

We turn our faces to the glow
recognise our temporary imprint
and resolve to make our way home

Pictures of you without me

When I see pictures of you
before we met
I see the lightness
the expectation
the optimism of a world unfolding
A world before

Then somewhere between a pantomime villain and cancer
I cast my shadow on your face
I know you are still there
and you would probably deny
anything but age and experience
pulling at your shoulders

but
when I see pictures of you
before we met
I wonder what pictures of you
would look like now
If we never had

The canals of Mars at their height

An empty bottle for bashing
better than any toy
You are in control
there is no pretence at role play

This is nature unreserved
You lean forward
your brim upturned
not only the sun lights your face

This is a choice
not a compromise
This is authentic
not a substitute or a version

Expressing, playing, stimming
whatever name I give it
is only my invention
and won't alter the fun one bit

If the bottle was made of precious metal
it wouldn't necessarily be any better
The red dust complements the bright blue
of living water

You are no longer apart from the topography

Man in a glass booth

I have a speck of dirt on my window
Outside the Channel contorts and wrestles

Inside I am consumed by the tiniest of smudges
obscuring my view
pulling focus
snagging

It's probably bird shit

Seagulls and crows
don't even pretend to
mock innocence
as they flirt with the invisible

Raw nature
in all its certainty and vigour
prevails
unwitnessed

What I need is a little sponge on a stick
I think you can get them at the Pound Shop

then we'll see

The smell of freshly cut grass is a communication

Lying flat on my lawn
the core pulling me in
I wonder what message
the blades are releasing

This morning I have no argument
with wasps or bees
or the spiders who web
the pagoda

I half bury a stray fig
to give it a fighting chance
Even the weeds are safe
hanging on to the soil for dear life

The September sun
blesses my skin
its rays colliding with oxygen
bruising the sky blue

I try to feel the Earth spin
against the clock
Humans are not built to lie on grass
too many knobbly bits

My head needs support

Pain is telling me something

I'm already at my computer typing

This is already memory

Twice as many hydrogen atoms as oxygen moving

I don't need to see his face to know it's him
the light has its own plans

In reality nothing is still as elements compete
A split second away there is another poem

If I want I can see a trail of silver
at the spill

or the ominous underbelly of distant concentrations
Everything I see is a reflection of this love

I can home in on the dislocation of arms
in motion

or glory in the contrast
of chemistry as liquid and gas

We may not see the same world at all
I hope yours is as full of splendour

> "And can you, then, who have such possessions
> and so many of them, covet our poor tents?" – *Caratacus*

With a narrowing of vision
the mountains could be envious of the sea
All that fluidity

Envy is usually selective
One could say it's a form of greed
or wishful thinking at best

It's not that the mountains
would want to stop being mountains
or lose their height and grandeur

They would only want to add
that extra something
they admire in the nature of water

There would be longing of course
and a feeling of inferiority perhaps
A resentment within the core

How could the mountains compete
other than with molten rock?
It would not be the same

Hiding guilt in those eyes
that avoid the waves and tides
It would never be the same

And to think once these mountains stood
so proud
the sky itself was envious

And if you
should lose your heart to the sea
how then should the mountains feel?

I'd like you to know

When you feel you've handled the situation
When you've used the jargon
    applied the textbook
When you've selected only the supporting facts

    edited memory and redrawn history
When you've ignored the question
    and deftly changed the subject

When you've gone on the attack
    to avoid the obvious
    and leave no space for reply
When you think you've got away with it

When you're patting yourself on the back
    for being so clever
        I'd like you to know I can see your lies

You've got me but who's got you?

Even the Earth moves
vulnerable in space
like an egg in a pinball machine

Lights and sounds distract our attention
from the lack of substance
like seatbelts on a fairground ride
inadequate if the ride goes off track

We hold onto each other
and force a brave face
so as not to frighten the kids

Time, rust, friction, wear and tear
and the bolt sheers

The best you can do is hope
and try to save others
Let your body break their fall

Christmas at the end of the world

It seems all old Portuguese men dress the same
as though they've come to a conclusion

At the end of the world
there is a chair so big
those that sit on it become children

The weight of the ocean
undercuts the candy-striped rocks
Termites in silhouette iPhone the sunset

In this place that others have called sacred
a light and mirrors safeguard invisible ships
waves move sideways on the lumpy horizon

The Earth spins on your finger
delicious and small
the universe is infant once more

Academia and the compulsion to compete

Too small to be a snowman
this could be a snowchild

I hold onto your hands
partly to warm them
but partly not

Two Brussel sprouts
a lemon for a nose
scarf and cap

We are not going to win any prizes
This is a family photo
of family
for family

It need be of no interest to anyone else
If you saw it in an album
you might well flick past without comment
a little embarrassed
that we would consider this worth presenting

Whether we are on a downhill slope
or uphill
is a matter of perspective

Our faces white as hoar frost
haunt these early learnings

When you were a baby
I put your name down for a school place
Paid a deposit

The money is no loss at all

Fame as a perpetual wedding

I've always hated shiny apple selfish people
whose lives are one big wedding
where they are the centre of attention

Their opinions
their qualities
their relationship

We bring them presents
we take their photos
we laugh at their speeches

we dress up, we wait
we clap, we cheer
we eat their stupid cake

we go home
and we give it six months

Audition for Heaven

I've been afraid
as long as I can remember

Not afraid of my brain becoming night
more afraid of failure

a particular failure
that of missing the point

I sometimes wonder if life actually exists
in the gaps between doing stuff

All the time spent waiting
and filling in

It would be ironic to arrive in Heaven
and find out

that
was the bit that mattered

then spend the rest of eternity
waiting and filling in

having
never quite mastered the art

Exploring rockpools

The surface
of an alien brain

Tie-dyed green
and glassy grey

Little pools of imagination
cloudy and mysterious

Step carefully
with feet bare

Miniature Loch Ness monsters
crowd the crevices

loose stones lurk
in murky salt water

We bend to connect
and there is treasure

for certain
there is treasure

The sea encouraging
at a distance

like a parent
ready to rush in

Horizontal amid horticulture

As I lower my head to the grass
I am shorter than the chives

Self-seeded fennel towers over me
like a monument to liberty

A cornflower weaves the trellis to gain height
Life is in competition for sunlight

The beech trees aren't big enough yet
to warrant the term trees

The poppies have lost their flowers
but not their sense of purpose

New blossom stands alongside those that wane
Passion flowers drape like curtains beside the swing

I am no threat to anything that crawls or flies
I am at a level with the salvias though not as attractive

Olive trees dominate the skyline
The sapling of a silver birch stands like an exclamation

Figs ripen at their own pace
drawing yesterday's rainfall upwards

Ornamental thistles brave it out amongst tall grasses
too regal to be mistaken as weeds

Unseen birds whisper secrets in Morse code

Faint clouds scour the sky like someone
hasn't rubbed them out properly

Wild mushrooms hide in the undergrowth
like lost golf balls

This season of new life

Nearby hawthorn bushes catch litter
blown from the beach

I pick them tidy
and carry the distraction

A thin skin of fresh green
now protects the Downs

There's a field for mothers
and their new born

a suspicion of rabbits
at pace

At the foot of the cliff
families watch their step

The tide is at its furthest reach
There is still a bite in the air

When the sun climbs
I am able to sit for longer

Though you are always more
than a name on a bench

touching the letters

is the nearest we can get
to an arm around the shoulder

Raining upwards

I have shrunk with age and grief
I am not sure I have a soul left to steal

He has his mother's nose
a family resemblance in outline

Our weather-proof coats
sort of match
hooded against the torrent

Deepest blue obscures into black
on the inside
the lack of detail gives the impression
my head exists in space
like a hologram
or a dark snow globe

The mountain behind looks unreal
a photoshop composite
complete with derelict shelter

Only his hand on my shoulder
instils solidarity
and cohesion

The hailstorm has all but subsided
leaving us a little bruised
and buffeted

There will be better days
and worse
for certain

It's in the nature of ice
when the stone grows too heavy
it cannot be sustained in mid-air

I look to you
for confirmation
I am still alive

Hominin footprints in Laetoli

Covered with earth to preserve
volcanic ash suggests that which is absent

A black and blue marble
forms the palest of lanterns

All we touch in this world
bears our signature

From a warm little pond
to the chemistry of consciousness

from bowing on all fours
we have raised our heads to the heavens

Far beyond the constellation in Hollywood concrete
there are trace fossils on the Sea of Tranquillity

As we teach each new child to stand
we move ever nearer the gods

Are other animals afraid of their own species?

Even on tip-toes the ceiling is too tall
though from a distance the halo we breathe
is nothing more than the shedding of outermost skin

Happiness is...

a trick played on you by your body
to encourage behaviour
beneficial to its survival

I've lived in fear all my life
Fear of change
or the lack of it

There is fear...
and there is lack-of-fear
We could call this happiness

Anger is fear
Sadness is fear
Surprise and disgust – all fear

Jealousy is fear...
When I was young I was angry at God
for not loving me as much as he did others

and if sadly he didn't exist then
I was angry at the universe for not loving me
as much as it did others

Pinning this cloud to the page
it appears to take up less space

Happiness is perhaps
an illusion of control
or an acceptance
of the lack of it

Electric like a tree praising the sky

I do a strange thing with
my head sometimes

I lift it up
raise my chin
look the world in the eye
defiant for no reason

This is who I am
this is what I am
deal with it

It's very unlike me

Deafness and social cohesion

I can't hear very well in restaurants
Let me clarify that

I can hear the background noise
just not the conversation
I'm supposed to be concentrating on

So people tell me jokes
and are disappointed by my lack of humour

Or proffer tough criticism
which I seem to take in my stride

Share secrets I never divulge

Ask me for things I never deliver
Questions I never answer

Make arrangements I never keep
Offer opinions I accept without argument

Evident

My wife has an eye for a photo
I am too conscious of duty
My father-in-law points the way
My son leans to be included
Only his grandma is camera ready
sunglasses on the top of her head
scarlet antlers marking the season
clashing with an array of pinks

I imagine a second image
like a spot-the-difference puzzle
where subtle changes are noted
My father-in-law facing forward
His wife not needing a seat
No bags under Angela's eyes
My hair without grey
Ear defenders no longer evident

There's more to lemons than being yellow

Alone with my lad and the waves
we brave the collapse of the cliff edge
A wading fisherman is bullied by the tides

There is a mist way out at sea
but the freshness on the margin
invigorates the skin

Debris around our feet
Life trying to keep hold
Lungs expand to fill all thought

I am here and consciously alive

We've crossed the line between
existence and exaltation
as though commonplace

Whether a shrine or a mirage
the shoreline is never long enough

Unmarked

A grave without a headstone
is just a scratch of ground

Overgrown
littered with autumn leaves

Easily mistaken for a short cut
Even the grave digger is embarrassed

Without tender husbandry

A gap in a row of teeth

Only recognised by the name
on the neighbouring plot

Somehow so different from ashes
scattered in a chosen setting

The absence lies within others

Naked before God
bare bones

left wanting

If you never saw this tree it must be difficult to imagine its glory

There is an absence of tone to my muscles
A lack of colour in my hair

We are in the Algarve off-season
across from where my wife buys gluten free

There is an absence of tree, unnoticed
Neither of us is native to this land

Unused chimneys on empty houses
are unconcerned

Even the surrounding grass is without life
the steps to the car park untrodden

Lines marking out unoccupied spaces
are unaffected

There is no wind to play with the palm leaves
now only imagined

There is nothing here to lean upon
On another day it stood taller than me by far

Now scissored cuts criss-cross the stump
there are no rings to confirm age

A lack of shade
filling the space of what once was

Soaking

Even in this late sun
it's a wonder my feet don't root
They are sodden

There's a leak somewhere around the nozzle
and I wrangle the hose
as gallons flood back finding a level

I like that watering forces me
to look at each plant
individually

My new drinking partners
sun-baked khaki
nurtured back to lush green

Glorying in technology
I adjust the spray to a fine rope
to reach the stragglers at the fence

A kink strangles the flow
and I smooth the loops
to restore the charge

I have a special attachment for the lawn
The twirl throws globules around like
a dog emerging from the sea

a dervish dance
the whiplash spitting
like a liquid spirograph

life restored
at the turn of a tap
Just a circular movement of the fingers

The self-deception of priority

I board the bus to the flight alongside the wheelchairs
and the families with small children
Mothers holding babies displace
elderly dads on the end seats

There's one arrogant-looking lone man
in his fifties who was first in the queue
and there's me

He looks the type that is used to getting
preferential treatment
and I worry I have that appearance
or indeed the attitude itself

I appreciate the irony as we stand and wait
for non-priority boarders to make up the numbers
before the bus heads off to the plane steps

Flying on my own always makes me self-conscious
I am redefined, no longer an elderly dad
already standing to leave seats free for families

The arrogant man leans back against the glass
and I see the outline of his out-of-shape stomach
against his tucked-in polo shirt

My polo shirt is untucked to avoid such unsightliness
My wife tends to book priority boarding
as a habit to head-off problems with our autistic son

Here now I look indulgent
like a businessman sneaked onto a flight
last minute by an overworked secretary

It would take too long
to explain to each and every passenger
and in the grand scheme of worries
I'm sure mine are not priority

The spiral staircase casts a shadow

Maybe there's a certain age
when you no longer fear skin cancer
where the sun is slight
its rays gratefully gathered in

A choice of vivid colour
widens the pupil
awake and vital
youth cramming the dial

The contrast of light and shade
like a before and after diagram
Yourself dark upon your work
or content without trace

The March of Progress

With respect to Rupert Salinger and Richard Dawkins

Evolution is only a straight line looking back
There is no one destination

Without guarantees
we step into the unknown
in all directions

From the age of reptiles
to the age of mammals

The selfish gene is not immortal
Fidelity is seldom total on
this entangled bank

This is what is
not what ought to be

We stumble, we fall, we fail
and we learn

Under gravity
we adapt to seasons and tides
through chance as much as design

We illustrate from this juncture
only what has survived

But in the richness of human culture
we carry the lives of those that falter

As again
we step into the unknown
in all directions

At the hearth of the winter sky

I put my faith in the automatic handbrake
and walk down the slope

You can take photos now directly at the sun
and although detail is obscure
silhouettes are epic against the falling star

We walk until there is only rock and waves
Looking back across the terrain
the scale is enhanced

Later waiting for a hot chocolate competes
against the final glory of refracted light

Sanctity in coral and ash

I try to catch the eye of the waiter
to register annoyance
but relent

Travelling in 4D

When my dad died
I was given his watch

Strange, as we never
spent that much time together
absent within the same room

Our days were marked by
coins stacked on the mantelpiece
electric, gas, bread and milk

I won't leave the watch to my son
he has no need to measure hours
Days are marked with meals and sleep

outside time or in perfect sync
A zone uncharted in any atlas

We are in the world as wide as it is
side by side

He chooses to walk with me
I choose to walk with him

With Johnny's arm around my shoulder
the spin of the Earth slows

Slitting my own throat

When I was a young man
I tried to shave all the beard from my face

Not just the hair I could see
but the hair I could feel

I scraped away again and again to remove any trace
any suggestion of shadow pending

What came was a huge rash
matted blood and rough skin

until I learnt
to cut the hair you can see

and be content that more
was to come

Auditioning for the X-men in the Wetlands

Drawn back to the lagoon
two shaved apes

neither of which speak the language
doing nothing much
not a thunderbolt in sight

This day wouldn't fill a postcard
The landscape lounges

We are happy mutants
sixty percent water
three percent orange juice

The sea and sky
an agreed grey

Elephant clouds
stepping the Pillars of Hercules
Pale amber kissing the dunes

The smile on my son's face
making the moment immortal

Without trespass

Your hands are together
as though in prayer

The image before you
has his arms raised
as though wanting to be picked up

Without trespass
I try not to project my hopes
and accept all possibility

Your hands might be caught mid clap
The image might be exalting the sky
You are more than my perception

You may be warming your hands
against the weather
The image may well be waving

You could be rubbing chalk between your palms
The image could simply be trying to surrender

Windswept and drunk on oxygen

                I sit with my dead brother
                      by the Atlantic
Two superheroes
disguised as my wife and offspring
try out their new costumes in the splash

                I wrap myself in my son's coat
                    the zip a Rubik's cube

We know the routine
fresh orange, side plate and olives
hold down the paper place mats
from the magpie wind

                  The tide edges into the river
                        reversing the flow

This moment is my life
My life is this moment

                    Soon it will be dark
              everything I now see will still be
                only with the absence of light

If I close my eyes
you are still here

Orphan

There is a plant in a pot separate from the garden

A cordyline with green and purple leaves
like a baby palm tree

It does not share the earth with the orange trees
or the spongy grass

Its soil now surrounded by terracotta
may well have originated from the bed nearby

but here roots are confined
nature contained

This individual adorns the patio no further
from the rest of life than you might scatter seed

Pilgrimage for the agnostic

It is reverence that marks the moment
To make time and space
religious or not
reflection brings you closer

In the want of a better place
I come to find something tangible beyond myself
though I know
this is not where you are
and is never where you were

Only your body is buried
in this formal row

You live within me

You have always lived within me
even before
Why then
would death change that

It is I myself
who have brought you here
and it is with me
you will leave

Headland

Our love is ahead of us
He walks the length of the beach without once looking back
Islets puncture excited turquoise
Jets scar the sky
comets with neutered tails

We are at the point where the earth moves
The vertical lines of rock
look like burnt toast on a rack
or black plates in a dishwasher

A breeze blows my hood at the back of my neck
With a trick of perspective
I hold the future in the palm of my hand

My boy hears music that I can't
he covers his ears

I am reflected in your eye

Guadalupe and the navigator

Trying to explain Jesus
to my son I realise
there is what I believe
and what I want to believe

These walls feel as old as hope
and my heart aches for a miracle
or the allowance
of the possibility of a miracle
somewhere
under the possibility
of Heaven

I wipe my eyes embarrassed as
my wife returns from the gift shop
leaflet in hand

The donkey we saw in the masonry
is a bull
to signify St Luke

The angels on the ceiling
slaves stolen by the infante

I give the guide to a young English man entering

I'm not aware if he has a son

This is the likeness of things that no longer exist

Those clouds you see
have long since passed

The horse has long since become glue
or dog food

Each leaf has been shed
each blade of grass grown out

This hair you see has long since
been swept from a barber's floor

The clothes either gone to charity
or the tip

Each cell of skin
has been replaced several times

Even the shadows on the soil
would no longer be cast the same

The sheet music of Microwave Background Radiation

Of course, the Big Bang was silent
as sound can't travel through a vacuum

In the afterglow
molecules formed
and vibrations rippled energy waves
light years in length

A cosmic chord
the scream of an infant birth
building into a deep rasping roar
and ending in a deafening hiss

Like a jet engine descending into TV static
The first tree falling in the forest unheard

The echo of this heavenly choir
deep below the octaves of the human ear
become bacterium on a bowling ball

At its smallest everything is sound
a universal string section
the DNA of reality

If you listen you can hear harmony
in the pulse of your blood

and the sadness of minor chords
heard by the first humans

Sand suspended in mid-air

Sand suspended in mid-air
defies the natural order

Johnny presses his teeth
against the back of his hand
to contain the excitement

My wife stands ready
as I bash the bottom of the
sun lounger once more

We can only see the effect
captured by a single frame

I'm unsure what delight
my son is experiencing

We can only see the effect
captured by a single frame

Eskimo kiss

One hand supports soft scalp
another removes all obstacles
you are safe again
surrounded by family

There is warmth in this welcome
gravity embraced
eyes lock and focus as never before
Generations whisper greeting

Biology reveals new sensations
a world immediate and infinite
Face to face with creation
you breathe the same air

Tiny fingers realise a first grip
am I part of you?
are you part of me?
there are no extremities today

Skin touching skin
a most human hello
essential learning
you are connected still

The foghorn has long since given up

Despite sea fret
Vitamin D warms my eyelids

The immediate is sharp
but distance bleeds into haze
like I'm inside a glass paperweight

Sitting on the terrace in my shorts
my bleach-white legs
stare out the UV rays

If you join the dots
on my limbs
a picture of psoriasis forms

Another gift passed down
from father to son

There's a fox that likes
to mark out his territory
in my garden
always on walls or steps
never on grass

If I put my knees together
and spread my feet apart
the rays can work
directly on the infection

My back will have to wait its turn
My black tea has now
ceased support

There's a green tinge
to the bones of trees

A hot shower this morning
has left my pores open
to all comers

A fly is drawn to the paraffin
on my head
I am expecting to spontaneously
combust at any time

A helicopter
rails against
the bird kingdom

Two tall chimneys
interrupt my view
They are for show only
but not from this angle

The February breeze
still has bite
Everything competes
to force my hand

I've other duties
and responsibilities
on the clock

If I half turn
I can see my phone screen clearer
in squat shadow

This may be the last of the sun
for a while
If I write a poem
I can hold on a little longer

What would I have done better?

My head is on upside down
Iron filings on opposite poles of a magnet

I can feel but I can't think
and even then it's confusing

Without imagination
monkey bars are just bars

Pyjamas, it appears, can be worn any time of day
Everything money can't buy I don't understand

I'm searching for clues in old memories
as if the answer was there all along

The world outside my brain is too big
in every direction

I could stare at yesterday forever
and still not understand

What would I have done better?
Everything

Exquisite

Against caution
you choose to be generous

Whether through habit or will
you seem at ease with giving

as though kindness was natural
as though empathy inbuilt

And while reality crowds our eyes
and frustration and greed stalk unfettered

you choose to open your arms
against all rationale

as though to convert the world
one at a time

I am besotted

The movement of shadows on the moon

Nowadays I find loading and unloading
the dishwasher a form of meditation

All news is weather
and I still wait for my real life to begin

Iridescent
It's the colour you don't see that's being absorbed

A different man stands before the ocean
skin as white as face cream

Only now this little bit of carbon
has finally forgiven God

I've learnt that the breastbone of an angel
needs to be far larger than mine

That once you're in the ground
you can't own your own grave

That blind mole-rats rub tears
over their body for defence

I am a man without a telescope
numbering the stars

My language is scraps
fallen from the grown-up's table

My regrets come so fast
they leave vapour trails

There's nothing I own
but these smudges of cloud

I have slept too long in one position

I've learnt Heaven doesn't solve
the need for meaning

it just shifts the location

First prize

As you climb the podium
we applaud
there is no grand speech

We are the only witnesses
if you discount
the shrubs and the sky of course

This is for fun
but motivation is there
balance and co-ordination

You are the hero
you have overcome
you are ready to play

There are no medals big enough
no metals shiny enough
to do you justice

Two wooden boxes
on a piece of grass
make you taller

But
you are already taller
you are already taller

You won't find a box to tick on any form for this

It must have taken some time to build that wall
and there are so many walls
and there've been so many lives spent building them

We sit together
our backs to the stones
each in our own breath

No-one can see what catches our eyes
only a quiet body language
You could be any teenager

I could be any dad
neither revealing superpowers of
good or evil

Your hand hovers
unconcerned with personal space
We are not afraid to touch in passing

We have arrived at an understanding
almost unnoticed
we are on the same side of the wall

This is merely blossom, fruit will follow

Palm trees know how to bend to a hurricane
and regain their shape

Unsteady
I spot-check my senses

My body creaks like these old sun loungers
The breeze is in danger of blowing my tan clean off

No matter how they itch
you should never scratch spots

You can scrape your nail around them
to ease the temptation and fool your nerve endings

Only on the final day of a holiday
am I about to relax

On a mountain of lemon trees
I sit on a bench at the bottom of the garden

and look back to where I live
like staring at myself from inside a mirror

The sun behind my shoulder
spoons like a lover

Leakage

I have one photo of you crying
a sole tear preserved in black and white
your cheek as yet soft canvas
sunlight surrounding your understanding

There appears a question
in the window of your eye
your pupil undilated
a confusion perhaps leaking out

This interaction is in close up
the background lacking focus
your pale lips unmoved
unable to control the tide

In the fifteen years since
you have not shed saltwater
on the outside
although

occasionally I catch the same look
on that same child face
only fleeting
as though unsure of the flood

There is a ghost on the shoreline taking a selfie

You are probably the only person
in that whole ocean
swimming with their 17-year-old son

The shape of the earth is shifting
Dry sand whisks around my feet

Diagonal lines in the cliff
show how once the land was at a different angle
before the world buckled and bent

There's a hazy cloud but with no edge
like a hollow fog

Thin trees on the slope lean south
A natural groyne lies like a brontosaurus on the beach

Black rocks skulk beneath the surf
volcanic sharks with unforgiving teeth

We are a line of shells at high tide
One ship is on the horizon
big enough to carry us all

Fresh air cocoons my brain
My eyes feel haunted

We eat olives and cheese before the main meal arrives

Fish heads stare at me from the side plate
They know I've put them at the corner of the table to distract the flies

The ship nears and veers away from the setting sun
a small boat in its wake

I am disguised as an old man trying to dress too young
I kiss the scars on my son's arms
and wonder what you see

As though infinity could be turned off

I watch as a small ball floats
blown by the breeze

It tours the ripples
and seems to come to rest
at the shallow steps

Then around again the current stirs and carries
this vulnerable toy
revolving green and blue
in and out of shade

The water's skin contorts
causing reflections to shiver
The wind plays peek-a-boo
A gust blurring the surface
like frosted glass

At the edge of the pool
droplets fall away
pulling on the strongest of bonds
atoms cascading after atoms
That weakest of powers, gravity
drawing everything closer

In my car at speed
I remember seeing water
climb the windscreen
as I accelerated
into rain
A temporary victory
almost as though I could outrun the universe

The difference between falling down and having a fall

I can no longer kid myself
that I've not peaked

My dad in the shaving mirror
can see through me

It's about mitigating the rate of decline
Matching an acceptance level

from the way up but without
the hope of better to come

I've fallen down many times
and picked myself up saying

"That's one less slip
that will catch me unaware

A useful education
A positive experience"

Then
there's having a fall
and seeing that long slope
stretching out before you

Whether a series of small but inevitable slips
    or one big fat fall from grace

        with each step
        I move ever nearer to

        the bruise that will never mend

Sofa at the centre of the constellation

You are easy with contact
body language like slang

Crimson girders
form a backbone

Worn leather
cushions the light

Cosmology and domesticity
seem strange bedfellows
but everywhere is local when you're there

We have put a hole in the ceiling
to let in the night

Heads tilted to the dark
we find ourselves in others

On one side a detailed history
cites the shades of the spectrum

We have travelled all the way to the moon
to discover the Earth

The walking wounded at Lidl

My psoriasis does not qualify
for priority parking

My wife eases her dodgy back
out of the vehicle

As eyes view us with suspicion
a blue badge authorises the windscreen

My father-in-law reveals nothing
of his need for statins

Only my mother-in-law looks the part
leaning heavily on her stick

A stroke and heart attack at the same time
qualifies her for a shorter walk to the supermarket

Earlier I saw her lift the weight from the world
Immersed in water

her limbs as free as summer
no time limitation in sight

Once inside the shop we are in public
A world of plenty is laid out before us

Fridges hum, tills bleep
muzak underscores decisions made

A little girl with no physical ailments
squeals constantly for attention
She too has her story

My son wears his ear defenders
as the two of us sit back in the car
out of the way
and wait

in the disability space

Vibrations

Electricity in the trees
Cicadas call to life

With some over a decade
in the dark
it's no wonder
they sing so loud

Dragging a needle
across vinyl
their song of courtship
can deafen the human ear

Seeking security in numbers
their only tactic
for immortality
is to overwhelm

When next
nymphs shed their skin
and brave the light
will I still have voice?

Earth reclaims the threshold

The door to the old house
has been retired to the garden
The pergola forming a frame
softened by variegated ivy

Unbolted, the oak wood opens
into a hidden corner where
a child's trampoline lies weathered
beneath neighbouring branches

Bamboo walls surround the nets
already going native
The dark beneath the springs
has become a cellar

There are new shoots amid rust
shrubs snuggling up
climbers reaching out
to lock elbows

Though I sense the spirit
of the law of nature
I don't have the language
to do justice to this fragrant anarchy

Still the door I recognise
functional and rectangular
crafted and domestic
not as yet buckled by the elements

The intoxication of tidal shift

From the outside a whirlpool
looks an impossibility

like the mapping of milk in coffee
but there is beauty in this energy

The simple draining of a bath
or the passing of an airplane

can curl the elements. My son
brings out the best in people

I see the curl in them
as he enters the room

as if he gives each permission
to be themselves

Before moving into the heart of a new lawn

If you look closely some strands of grass
are far longer than others

The darkness of my jeans absorbs the light
heating my thighs like a radiator

I have a windmill that turns in two different directions
like the minute and second hands on a clock at odds

This is a bench in my garden
I've never sat on before

Halfway down the brick steps
like raked theatre seating

Green in many shades is becoming overgrown
Honeysuckle entangles a metal sculpture

Birdsong loops and rises
Clouds on high lay dissipated like flour through a sieve

I have memories in this space from early fatherhood
climbing frames, splash slides, inflatable pools

ponds of frogspawn and water lilies covered with wire
all now landscaped out of mind

Landed

Once in my shorts I'm officially on holiday

Fishing stray palm leaves
with the pool net is therapy

almost an ancient mystic art
requiring meditation and oneness
with chlorinated water

the resistance to the pole at depth
loops and curls the current

sleeping snakes stir
contort and evade
to no avail

There is a satisfaction in returning
each leaf to the garden with a little jolt
the ghost hood inside out

Also a satisfaction
in the pure blue of the pool
without distraction

balance restored
for a moment

A small corner of the world as it should be

The shaded garden

Some of these plants could be weeds
Some are exotic

The bamboo I recognise
It has outgrown me and then some

The Japanese acer stands delicate in the corner
its leaves like ornamental copper

Assorted trees and hedges on the south border
have become one, imitating jungle

the track of the lawn mower the only sign of civilisation
Kamikaze wasps patrol

Slugs have left little leaf on one poor plant
the remains – a dying stencil

A lighter acer edges the pergola
looking like an oriental side dish

There is a small wooden hut
almost a hidden temple

Climbers hang across the doorway so
you have to bow as you enter

Kissing the top of my own head

Everyone says I look like my uncle John
only not yet as old

He once told me
of the worst day in his life
and it was the same as mine

I kiss the top of my son's head

I'm not sure where we are
but those are my lips
and that's Johnny's blond hair
and that's all that's needed

I remember my uncle John
kissed the urn as he
scattered my brother's ashes

After that
how could I not
hug this man

There are layers of cloud moving in diffcrent directions

As the wave retreats
it catches the pebbles
like the keys of a musical box

This scree on the foreshore
becomes like a cheese grater for water
The sound almost a small round of applause

Each wet stone blinks a glint of sun
before the next surge
towards my abandoned clothes

A short walk west
there is a pregnant woman in the sea
possibly eight months swollen

Her partner and two toddlers
at her side
on an invisible cord

At this distance
they could be any nationality
speak any language

Light rolls on each undulation

In the background
a row of headlands
line up to bless the ocean

This is a photo of me not smiling

I have been taught
not to smile

I haven't been taught
what to do instead

So what we have
is an absence of smile

This is a photo of me
not smiling

This is a photo of my body
not smiling

This is a photo of the outside
of my body
not smiling

I've no recall
of what is happening inside
and no photo to help me

A little slope of meadow outside my window

It's only mid-May but the snowball tree
is past its best

The dragonflies have left and
only the wood pigeons and a few friends
insist on being noticed

The magnolia is already saving itself
for next spring
The wind has blighted the upper leaves

With cherry blossom now long gone
the main tree stretches out for sunlight
and makes the most of its shaggy haircut

In between the red bricks of the car port
small scraps of green blotch like
felt tip on graph paper

at the bottom of the bank the grass is thicker
a scouting party of daisies appear diffident
There's a sole dandelion feigning innocence

A squat dwarf willow crouches like a country hat
My wife wants to put two cartoon eyes on it
to make it a muppet

At a discreet distance a thin tree with paler leaf
is propped by a wooden post
a few branches don't have any foliage at all

This latest addition appears healthy but almost
like life is drawing straws

Altamura Neanderthal

An old European cousin entombed
biology now chemistry
more cave than man

Amid stalactites
and stony globules
as though bejewelled

hollow red eyes seem to plead
for lids to bring back the darkness

Experts fear rescue lest he fractures
Lazarus in limestone

He has no descendants to mourn him
you can hurt him no more
let him sleep
let him dream

The stone mask

Through this likeness
I validate my claim

I identify with the ancient
the unimpeachable authority

My human features mock
the spectre

More than a face
I am healed-blank

Transformed
invulnerable

All controls suspended
God-like

with deliberate intent
I am emergent

Naked as I am
beneath
I am no longer afraid

I've never had an email worth keeping forever

I have a letter rack
with no letters in it

It used to hold bills
but never a letter

Why I've acquired it
and why I keep it at all
these are both mysteries

If I get a letter
or several letters
I do have somewhere to put them

So I entertain at least
the possibility
of getting a letter

a letter worth keeping

Reclaimed

My camera can't capture the breadth
of this wind-teased ocean
or the authority of volcanic mounds
that fall away far beyond the beach

180 degrees of untamed depth
180 degrees of fire made solid

Johnny pinches his mum's skin
playful in this physical domain

Small barnacles polka dot
black boulders on the beach
smoothed by abrasion

All this ground upon which I stand
is just a bigger rock rising out of the sea

I am anchored in the present by family
We whoop and shout into the high wide sky

For a full 360 degrees our world
remains beautifully autistic

Pivot

Looking back at my new home

the grass slope tilts the bench
a little like a dentist's chair

The solar panel on the reclaimed slates
resembles a minimalist painting

There is more in the air
than you might first imagine

The baseline from the road
dulls as it bends over and round the trees

In my son's window the backs of nutcrackers
parade as triangle, the tallest in the centre

I can see my usual seat on the terrace
now high above my head like a thought bubble

I am avoiding responsibility
hoping to justify my absence

by filling the moment with
the pause untaken

the sky is blueberry ice cream

Self-portrait of the poet as an old man

I point my spots accusingly
at the sun

As I drink water
my corrugated fingertips smooth

I feel it won't be long
before I leave this precious flesh

I can't remember the numerous times
I had sex in my youth

but I remember the times
I was certain I felt love

I could be obscure here
as a means of protection

but the truth of this communication
is

I am now the age my brother was
when he died

It occurs to me
the greatest tribute
I can pay him
is to live the kind of life
I wanted him to have

A victory of sorts
Each day a battle hard won

For him
I wanted so much

Near miss

North towards the Bay of Biscay and home
I am in stasis

At high altitude
the view down from the plane
is like looking through a microscope

An alien underworld
of random lines and patches of colour

An eggshell tapped with the back of a spoon
Algae forming in furrows
Lakes like spilt ink

Scrapes of snow
where perhaps a giant has pulled his boots
across the summit

until in peripheral vision
the coast surprises
littered with dust from broken tiles
A straight line drawn with the wrong hand

Then
arcing over the water
a wagon train of clouds head west

White flecks in the deep blue confuse
An inversion of space

Lifting my head in reflex
for an instant I see other lives
pass in the opposite direction

Despite our relative speeds
almost in slow motion
other eyes catch mine

Considering all that exists in three dimensions
and the amount of time in any one life
and given the ability to alter speed, height and direction
you would hope
collisions would never occur accidentally

I look around for reassurance
teenagers submitting to screens
parents policing infants
all oblivious to the closeness of the inevitable

The cabin staff retain their fixed smiles
There's a curtain across the front of the aisle
that's not fooling anyone
like a dishcloth trying to cover a windshield

and I wonder if each pilot saw
the surprise on the other's face

later
as we land
all my problems
become my problems
again

Hold me with certainty in this heavenly chaos

Lead me by the hand
to where pirates sleep

where air has crossed the sea
to find me

where my skin shines
and my lungs draw deep

and leave all fear and doubt
behind me

Late renewal

Speeding on the way to the cemetery
I'm thinking about overtaking a hearse

I console myself in that
there's a set time period in which to receive a ticket

And I wasn't going to write any more poems about death
although I do love the words 'bone garden'

Even today
I can't bring myself to take out gravestone insurance
It smacks of a lack of faith

I park in the marked area
outside the gates

and hope no-one breaks in
whilst my mind is elsewhere, off guard

Removing old flowers and dusting the stone
gives me an excuse to stroke the grave
run my fingers along the words
and numbers that go back a lifetime

I break open the plant food
that makes the new flowers last longer
though I know
no-one will be there to see them

No-one but the deceased that is
and that's who they were for anyway

Witness

This is a tree that knows me
I played under its branches as a child

Its weathered trunk may well be heavier
but these longer limbs can still embrace

Its shadow has stretched in the late afternoon

Though all around has been relabelled progress
it has set itself in this fickle landscape and
reached an accommodation with the sky

Of course, the sun is the same sun
but it has no sense of loyalty

There is commitment with a tree

This is an old friend
that knew well
those we've lost

When I'm gone
it will still know

and it will remember
that I spoke of you

Moon in the morning sky

Like a dinner guest
still there at breakfast

Its appearance is the same
only the context has changed

easily mistaken for a small cloud
but for the expanse of clear blue

Reflected light marks
half its full shape

To complete the picture
requires imagination

or a memory of what was once revealed
or at least basic understanding of geometry and cosmology

It sits in the west
in no hurry to slip away

I am the only living thing in my garden
not facing the sun

The blanket of green surrounding me
varies in detail at closer inspection

Deep reds and burnt orange
fight for attention

Tiny blue-purple buds emerge
as though a little shy

Olive green is easily distinguished
Bushes and shrubs soon stand out

like when concentrating on the hard bits
of a jigsaw puzzle

Each leaf is a child's drawing
Shapes and sizes now too obvious to have been missed

Small birds insist it's morning
A digital alarm that won't be muted

The wind strokes my hair

The moon has definitely moved
in relation to the yardstick of the tall cactus

Now lower in the sky
it nears the top of the distant roofs

It seems only by looking away
distracted for a moment
can I perceive movement

I feel a warmth at the back of my neck
as I watch the slowest of goodbyes